How to be Heard in a Noisy World

How to be Heard in a Noisy World

Church publicity made easy

PHIL CREIGHTON

Authentic

LONDON ● ATLANTA ● HYDERABAD

First published in 2007 by Authentic Media

13 12 11 10 09 08 07   7 6 5 4 3 2 1

First published 2006 by Authentic Media
9 Holdom Avenue, Bletchley, Milton Keynes, MK1 1QR, UK
285 Lynnwood Avenue, Tyrone, GA 30290, USA
OM Authentic Media
Medchal Road, Jeedimetla Village, Secunderabad 500 055, A.P., India
www.authenticmedia.co.uk

British Library Cataloguing in Publication Data
A catalogue record for this book is available from the British Library

ISBN-13: 978-1-85078-716-7

Cover Design by MOOSE77
Typeset by Waverley Typesetters, Fakenham
Print Management by Adare Carwin
Printed and Bound in the UK by J.H. Haynes & Co., Sparkford

CONTENTS

ACKNOWLEDGEMENTS

Writing a book is a team effort: while the author gets all the credit, there are a band of unsung heroes who are working behind the scenes to help. And the biggest help has been my wife, Judith, who – even though we've only been married a few months – gave her blessing to let me write in all my spare moments. Likewise, Mark Woods, editor of *The Baptist Times*, deserves thanks for being so understanding while I've been writing. Andrew Waugh, pastor of Wycliffe Baptist Church in east Reading has been invaluable for bouncing ideas off, Peter Lowman, another pastor at my church, has been willing to pray for me and offer his support. Charlotte Hubback and the team at Authentic Media are great. Matt Bugg has been a great help with pictures and diagrams.

Support and encouragement has also come from Ali Hull, Andy and Eleanor Thomson, Russ Bravo, Tom Sandars, Richard McKenzie, Fenton and Cath Wallace, Ruth Dickinson and

Daniel Grote, among others. I strongly believe that this book is a ministry, and I encourage you to pray for other churches as they read it, ask God to open their hearts to taking publicity seriously.

Other thanks and acknowledgements: James Ashford, Roger Anderson, BBC, Colin Brodie, Jason Cheswick, Yvonne Coppock, Dagenham Baptist Church, Infront, Clive Jarvis, Robert Jones, McDonald's, Shell, TV Licensing, Mark Passenger, John Rackley, Paul Sinclair, Sky, Gordon Thorn, and to the people who have kindly lent their faces for the photos.

INTRODUCTION

Churches are fantastic, offering so many different things to their local communities – be it social action, pastoral care, youth clubs, safe havens for homeless people or even serving a pensioners' luncheon. You can probably rattle off a good dozen facilities that your fellowship provides. Despite this, we have a tendency to let our churches remain unsung heroes. Congregations are made up of all sorts: rich and poor; young and old; well and ill. We're a place for the misfits and we're a bit of a rag-tag army because 'while we were still sinners, Christ died for us'.

So, given our desire to make people's lives better and give meaning to their lives, why is it that church attendance is plummeting? Why do some people think the Church is boring and a waste of time? And why do some churches think that they're the rearguard action in a world that thinks Christianity's for wimps, the old or children? The answer is simple: we're not very good at blowing our own trumpets – after all, all the glory for what we do should go to God.

Statistics make depressing reading. Seven million people currently attend church on a Sunday and that figure is one of decline. Christian Research suggests that church attendance in 2040 will be just two per cent of the UK population. And yet, when it comes to the important things in life – births, marriages and deaths – people are still turning to the church. People want God to be part of their lives, but the size of the part he's offered varies. Perhaps because of this, some churches expect the world to come to them, instead of fulfilling the Great Commission to 'go and make disciples of all nations, baptising them in the name of the Father and of the Son and of the Holy Spirit' (Mt. 28:19).

Visiting churches around the country, I feel that they think that they are under siege and facing an uphill struggle to fit in with our contemporary, post-modern, post-irony, new-wave, integrated, multi-faith society, where wicked is good, and pants is bad. But, 'Jesus Christ is the same yesterday and today and for ever' (Heb. 13:8) – the power of the Gospel message has not been diluted even though the world we live in has changed. It's the way in which we promote the Gospel that has to change and, in the twenty-first-century West, that means introducing a form of marketing and perceiving Church to be a brand, no matter how uncomfortable this concept seems.

If the Church is going to get its message across (that Jesus changes lives), then we need to look at ways of getting that message heard. It's time to get away from truly terrible and sub-standard day-glo posters with cheesy slogans. With new technology making it easier to produce professional publicity materials on a budget, we've never had a better opportunity to update the image of the church and in doing so transform people's perceptions of us and the Gospel message.

And that's what *How to be Heard in a Noisy World* is about. The book is a unique toolbox looking at everything that a visitor to your church will notice. It's a guidebook for anyone looking for help with their church signs, with the way in which they welcome visitors to services and when they talk to the media.

Over the following pages, we'll go on a journey that will transform your church: it's my vision to see every church in the country growing and thriving because they're making disciples. Not all the advice will be applicable to your situation, but a lot of it can be adapted to suit your fellowship.

And the book isn't the end of it. Log on to

www.ditchthedayglo.co.uk

and you'll be able to access more advice and discussion forums where ideas from different churches can be shared, offering mutual encouragement. Working for the Kingdom business means working together: our key aim is to go and make disciples. It's an awesome responsibility given to us by Christ, but let's get his life-changing message heard in a noisy world.

ONE

VISION ON: CREATING A MISSION STATEMENT FOR YOUR CHURCH

What is the Church here for? More to the point, what is your church here for? Why have people gathered in your church for goodness knows how many years? And why does the general public have completely the wrong end of the stick about church and Christianity? For the majority of the UK, church plays no part in their lives. The 2001 Census revealed that more than 71 per cent of the country considered themselves to be Christians, yet the nation's pews are filled by just 7 per cent of the UK population – and that figure continues to decline. Something is wrong. Our life-changing message is not getting across and it is not being understood.

If you ask a non-Christian why they don't go to church, they might say: it's dull, it's boring, it's cold, it's old-fashioned, it's irrelevant, it's untrue, Christians put me off, sermons are useless, pews are uncomfortable or you don't need to go to church to be a Christian. These clichés came from my non-Christian friends. Some of their comments were harsher: 'If I want to listen to someone talking twaddle and people singing awful songs, I can stay at home and watch *Pop Idol*.' We've got a bad press, well deserved, as we've perfected 'meek and mild' in the bland and inoffensive sense.

But I believe that people do want to go to church – another said, 'You look at, say, the church scene in *The Blues Brothers* and think "I'd go to that."' A church that is alive – not necessarily lively – is a church that will attract people who are seeking their missing spiritual dimension. A church that doesn't even know what it's there for is one that will continue to perpetuate the clichés.

To make your church attractive, you need to start with the basics. It's a given that you're there to worship God, to encourage people to have a personal relationship with Jesus and that God's help for us today is the Holy Spirit. If your church is to revolutionise its publicity, then it must have a purpose and sense of mission. This clearly defined aim must be something that the whole fellowship can agree, work and aspire to. In normal, everyday speak that's a mission statement.

Some companies use their mission statement to set out their vision and how they intend to achieve it. Here, as an example, is Easyjet's:

> *To provide our customers with safe, good value, point-to-point air services. To effect and to offer a consistent and reliable product and fares appealing to leisure and business markets on a range of European routes. To achieve this we will develop our people and establish lasting relationships with our suppliers.*

It's straightforward: it wants to provide good customer service by offering a reliable and cost-effective service, provided by motivated staff and long-term business relationships with suppliers. If you've watched *Airline*, you'll have seen how the company's staff tries to help its customers. Indeed, the flights I've taken with them have been enjoyable. For me, this mission statement is a reliable indicator of the company's values.

Having a mission statement won't make you more media savvy, nor should it affect the Gospel message you preach – but it will help give you a sense of direction that will help plan your outreach and publicity. Without going through these steps, you will find reasons for publicising your church much harder.

Producing a church mission statement

Mission statements and slogans will take time to get right. Churches need to ensure that their members can agree with it and not sign up with gritted teeth.

Here's the mission statement for Wimborne Baptist Church in Dorset.

- To love and worship God
- To love and serve one another, our local neighbourhood, and the wider world
- To live and speak the good news of Jesus Christ, so that others become his disciples

Like all good sermons it contains a three-point plan. In this case, it's about how this church intends to be. Anyone reading it will instantly have a flavour of the fellowship: it is a missionary church that promotes God's love through its actions.

The Revd Robert Jones, the church's pastor, said: 'It was the result of quite a long and painful vision-seeking process. We answered the following questions: who are we meant to be; what are we meant to do; and how do we do that?'

To produce a mission statement, set some time aside in leaders' or parish council meetings. Ask the congregation to pray for leadership from God about the direction he wants the church to head in. Be prepared to fast to hear his voice. Get the church leadership team to walk around the neighbourhood, looking for specific needs that your fellowship can meet. Is there a homeless problem? Is there a toddlers' group? Is it an area of poverty? Are large houses fenced off and neighbours don't know each other?

You'll also need to decide how you want your church to be perceived. Are you completely against any form of modernisation? Do you want people to come to worship in their Sunday best, or their comfortable clothes? Are you prepared to let people fall in the Spirit? And is your communion called Holy Eucharist? Work out the answers to questions of this ilk and add them to the information about the neighbourhood you serve.

You will probably have to spend a long time discerning the type of church that God wants you to be. This book isn't to give you advice on this: it assumes that, as long as you have looked at the area you serve, the church you are now and the church you believe God is calling you to be, you will be able to formulate a mission statement.

There is no point in deciding that your mission is to bring young people to Christ if you're surrounded by retirement flats; likewise, if your church is in the middle of a housing estate where there are no activities for young people, it is a waste of resources to concentrate on a ministry to the homeless.

An ideal statement should be three sentences or less, describing the church's responsibilities to the people it intends to reach out to and church members should be able to use it as guidance for the way in which they implement the church's vision. Spend time drafting the right wording, look at other mission statements; they shouldn't boast, but be full of aspiration. Choose the words carefully – tighten each sentence so they're easy to remember. Spend time in a church meeting discussing it in small groups and ensure that the church is in favour of it.

Once you have a mission statement, and it has been agreed, let every church member have a copy. When people join the church, in addition to any statement of beliefs you may have, ensure that they receive a copy of the mission statement. And, of course, don't let this statement be binding: revisit it on a regular basis to ensure you continue to meet the changing needs of your community.

The slogan

Your mission statement can be used as a starting point for a church slogan which can be used with your logo (see chapter 2). Slogans are memorable, as these golden oldies prove: a Mars a day will help you work, rest and play; you go to work on an egg; a brand of toilet paper is soft, strong and very long; you know who makes exceedingly good cakes; and you buy a range of beauty products because you're worth it ... Valerie Noble's essay 'The Psychology of the Slogan' in *The Effective Echo: a Dictionary of Advertising Slogans* (1970) points out that:

> *Within the functions of memory, the slogan acts as a handle. It is a mnemonically structured device which is a conscious or unconscious effort to hook into the reader's subconscious. Used effectively, it can succeed as no other single element in advertising can.*

People remember slogans and the brand that they represent. Their power should therefore not be underestimated.

One church's solution is 'Good news for Collinstone'. It's a positive slogan: Collinstone Community Church is good news for Collinstone: it wants to be a force for good in the town. But the church offers Good News for Collinstone, relating the slogan back to the witness part of the mission statement.

You might be tempted to use a Bible verse, but with more than 31,000 to choose from it's tricky. For many people, seeing Scripture is an instant switch-off: especially when some churches insist on using posters displaying Bible verses in old English: 'The blood of Jesus Christ cleanseth from all sin.' It means nothing to me, so what does it mean to those fluent in txtspk? In an ideal world, where everyone knows the Bible, using Scripture would be right. I'm not denying the power of God's Word – I just don't think it's usually suitable for a slogan.

Brainstorm some ideas: sometimes the right idea will come straight away, but often it will take some wordplay, some sketching and some talking. Go back to the lists you drew up for your mission statement. Write down things that you'd like to be known for, such as praying, helping, loving, caring, serving etc. Write down some facts about the church's situation: neighbourhood, town centre, urban, rural, village. Think of other words you might want to add to your list – evangelism, Gospel, God's love, etc. Remember, there is no single right answer here; each church needs to define a slogan that is both unique and true to its situation.

You might be able to coin a phrase that is just right: 'the church on the corner' is memorable, but 'the church at the crossroads' pictures an indecisive fellowship that doesn't know where it's going. One slogan I used is 'come and ask questions' – which is very bold, as it's an invitation that suggests to the public that the church has answers, even though all it has is biblical truth. The Jesus Army lists on its website one slogan which you might aspire to: 'fighting for the poor, deprived, rejected, marginalised'. It suggests a church that is determined to make a difference, but it could be read as an aggressive stance rather than a positive one.

From your brainstorming, you should be able to devise a good selection of possible slogans. Some will have more potential than others; some will need polishing. Take them to a church meeting; let the members loose on the suggestions, making amendments and reaching agreement on which is the right one.

Producing a mission statement and slogan isn't an attempt to turn your church into a corporate enterprise, offering a production line approach to winning disciples. While they will help a church focus on its mission, it won't help a congregation cope with the problems we face being a church.

If you've thought that you don't need to have a statement or slogan, then think about the Cheshire Cat in Alice in Wonderland: if you don't much care where you want to get to, 'then it doesn't matter which way you go.' Having a sense of direction will help you plan your publicity, as you have a purpose and a focus. We can't afford to have fellowships that don't know where they're going.

TWO

WELCOMING BRANDING: FORMING A CORPORATE IDENTITY

If a mission statement helps churches focus on their mission, a church's corporate identity (its logo, its usage and the typefaces) that's in keeping with the statement will help a church communicate its message. The identity is important because we are instinctively visual: we remember images far better than text. Research proves this time and again – a 2004 survey of seven thousand people in six countries, found that McDonald's golden arches and Shell's pecten shell were recognised by 84 per cent, while 54 per cent could identify the cross.

In the Channel 4 series *Priest Idol*, a marketing company, Propaganda, developed a corporate branding for the parish church of Lundwood, renaming it *Church Lite*. The company said, 'Research within the parish showed that many people felt that church was stuffy, preachy and boring. The brand removed these negative aspects and communicated how the church can actually provide a solution to people's everyday problems.' And it worked: a marketing campaign using the *Church Lite* branding increased attendance dramatically and changed the village's perception of church overnight.

Steve Dixon, Propaganda's executive creative director, said: 'The church is simply the biggest brand that exists. The church must take on the responsibility of breaking down barriers and find a way to communicate with modern society.'

If branding is so powerful why do so few churches use it? Probably because so few people have thought about using it, often preferring to use the name of the church in bold lettering, a picture of the building or a denominational logo. These are instantly forgettable and don't tap into the biggest brand that Steve Dixon alludes to. Branding is also possibly ignored because it has to be secondary to the Gospel message that a church preaches.

Think about where your church could use a logo. At first, you might come up with just a letterhead. But there's also display boards, business cards, newsletters, notice sheets, OHP slides, TV monitors, websites, clothing, leaflets, press releases, sermon notes, rotas, name badges, handbooks, mugs ...

One key reason for using a logo across this range of material is for consistency: it suggests a church that is working together with the same vision for sharing the Gospel. It's possible to see this as a straightjacket, forcing everyone from the Sunday school leaders to the women's fellowship to follow a set of rules. But with the right set of guidelines they become a useful tool.

Definitions

A **corporate identity** refers to the way in which logo and accompanying typefaces are used. A **logo** refers to a unique design that sums up the essence of a company or, in our case, a church.

What makes a good logo?

What makes a good logo? The Shell pecten and McDonald's arches should give a clue: without words, they graphically convey the company. They are simple design shapes seen the world over. The McDonald's logo doesn't contain any references to the fast food industry it represents, and the Shell pecten has nothing to do with petrol. The obvious choice for designing both logos would be something related to the industry in which it works – a burger and an oil well. Applied to churches, it means you can avoid using a cross or a fish, both visual clichés that might conjure up images of sandal wearing Bible-bashing Christians.

Both logos also work in colour and in black and white (mono). Shell has a mono version of its pecten to be used in such circumstances. Your church logo similarly will be more versatile if you have both. It might help you to design the logo in mono first and then add colour.

Getting ideas

Look around for ideas: tear out logos you come across in magazine adverts, letterheads, Internet sites, packaging and newspapers. But don't look at what other churches are doing, as you should produce something unique to your fellowship. If your church building is distinctive, such as a listed building or in a picturesque location then it might be appropriate to use a drawing of it for your logo.

Let a designer do the design work

Your logo needs to be the best; while you might have someone in your fellowship who is a graphic designer, it's highly likely you won't. If this is the case, be prepared to spend money commissioning a designer to create a logo for you. For small churches, this might seem like an unnecessary expense, but it will be worth it as it will be used a lot. If you can use a Christian designer, they might be able to give you a discounted rate. Brief them thoroughly as they need a clear idea of what you want. Give them your mission statement and slogan, a list of the church's activities; explain whether you are a traditional or modern fellowship. They need to know all kinds of extra information, such as the colours you feel represent the church (is it warm, friendly, modern, eye-catching etc.) and whether you wish to project a traditional or up-to-date image using modern typefaces. Encourage their questions, invite them to visit, or take pictures during a service. Let them get a real flavour for your fellowship: if you were a stick of seaside rock, they'd want to know what lettering would run through it.

The cost for this design will vary according to the time it takes to produce, but you can help cut down on idea generation by deciding some of the things that you'd like in the logo. For example, if your church is in an arable farming community, it might be appropriate to incorporate images such as a wheatsheaf. A city church aimed at young professionals might choose to use heads of church members as examples of the typical congregation. You might want something clever done with the initials, or use an image of your church's skyline. The only limit is your imagination.

However, the created logo must give value for money: having a long shelf life (at least a decade to make the expense justifiable). The best logos, such as Coca-Cola's, are timeless. It must be usable at different sizes: the size of your thumbnail to foot-high letters on a billboard. You might want it to convey emotions, something the cuddly Michelin Man does, or identify yourself without words, such as the Nike tick. Finally, ensure that the designer gives you copies of the logo at different sizes in different file formats: TIFFs, JPEGs etc.

Designing a logo

Here's the current logo for Collinstone Community Church. It takes a cross from a clip art collection and uses some ordinary typefaces to spell out the church name and looks amateurish.

It's possible to make this mundane logo better, simply by deleting the 'CCC' and setting the name of the church in full:

The cross continues to make this look cheap: if anyone can recreate a logo, then it's not unique. So, using a computer illustration programme, we can create a 'hand drawn' cross:

This transforms the logo, turning it into a design with its own distinctive image. However, the church name is bold and lost in space. Let's move it and change the typeface so it's softer:

This sets a very different tone for the church, especially if compared with the first version. Choosing the right typeface is important, as you automatically use the style to determine the type of church. The following examples each use a different typeface – see how your perception changes.

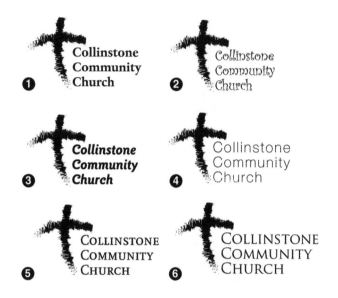

Choosing the right typeface for your church is important as it says so much about you. Of the six examples above, number 2's curly writing is unsuitable for a church: it's frivolous. Number 4 is quite clinical, because it uses a thin sans serif typeface. Number 6 has authority thanks to its classical lettering. The other examples are warmer in tone – would any suit your church?

But we want to get away from a cross, even a unique one as seen above. And a logo is a good place to incorporate a slogan (the mission statement distilled into a few words). Collinstone's logo needs to convey a dynamic, modern fellowship that emphasises its Christian ethos and incorporates its slogan 'bringing the community together', the role that the church sees for itself: a focal point for the neighbourhood. This led to the idea of the community and church being in God's hands.

Bringing the community together

The swirl indicates a dynamic church and that it's in God's hands. This can then become part of the church's corporate branding – placed discreetly on the bottom right hand of a sheet of paper, used on name badges (see below) etc.

The name of the church is in a contemporary typeface – Officina Serif Bold – and a drop shadow behind it adds a 21st century feel. The slogan is in the italic version of Officina Serif, offering a complementary touch.

To help visualise the difference to an identity that subtle changes can bring, here are three more versions of the same logo, but using Comic Sans, Arial and Times New Roman – all common typefaces – and a simple curved line.

Bringing the community together

You can see the difference between the different settings –
compared to the professional logo, they look bland and dull. By
changing the curved line to a thick line, it now looks more like
a smile than a visual representation of God holding the world
in his hands. But it is the choice of typeface that is crucial to
the identity of a church, and all churches need to understand
how typography works in order to use it well. A brief guide
appears as an appendix at the end of this book. It's worth
mentioning here that you should avoid the above typefaces
in your work (Comic Sans, Times New Roman and Arial) as
they are typographical clichés in the sense that everyone uses
them. Comic Sans particularly stands out as a typeface that is
not suitable for anything other than a clown's convention and
should never be used in church work.

Drawing together a corporate identity

Now we have a logo and chosen some appropriate typefaces, we
need to return to devising a corporate identity for your church. A
church is a collective of Christian believers, brought together to
serve and worship God – in many ways it's a ragtag army rather
than a streamlined business. However, by establishing some
design ground rules in the form of a corporate identity, you can
give your fellowship a house style for its communications that
helps church members understand publicity. Establish design

rules by producing a style guide, a short document detailing the how, when and where of your church's identity. Copies of this can be given to those in the fellowship that need it. The style guide is always a work in progress as circumstances change; viewing the style guide as an inflexible friend will let you become its slave. To get an idea for what a style guide can be like, it's worth searching for 'corporate identity guidelines' on an Internet search engine. You should find style guides from a range of different organisations, giving you a good feel for what they say.

What questions does the style guide need to answer?

- *How should the logo be used?* When is it appropriate to use? Where should it be positioned on a page? How large should it be? Can it be used in different colours? What are the colours used in the logo?

- *Which typefaces are used to accompany the logo?* A church should choose two typefaces for its identity: a serif for using in letters, notice sheets, etc., and a sans serif for headings, signs, name badges, as a secondary typeface. These faces should complement the logo and each other. You'll know if they work together if they look right together: you should only notice typography if it's bad typography.

- *How large should these typefaces be used in correspondence such as letters?* Word processing programmes default body copy to 12 points, so the temptation is to use it at 12 points. However, with the right line spacing and margins, you can comfortably use 10 or 11 point text. Experiment with different settings.

- *What margins should be used in word processing programmes?* Once you have experimented with the necessary margins (remember: no more than 12 words per line) then you need to create a template. Word processing programmes are designed to do this easily and the advantage is that instead of overwriting a previous document, every time you open the template it creates a new document which you have to save. This can include the church's logo.

- *How should these typefaces be used in other church documents?* Are they essential in, say, letters to parents of youth group? Using to project words on to the large screen?

- *What about the Internet?* You can use the church identity in banners, buttons and navigation bars.

- *What kind of image does the church want to portray to the community by implementing this style guide?*

In some circumstances, it's worth ignoring your guidelines; they have to be used at your discretion. Keep an eye on the latest technology and design trends; be prepared to keep up with the times to show that the Church is still relevant today.

Why corporate identities matter

You might think that getting to grips with corporate identities and typography is a waste of time as it doesn't help share the Gospel. But it's part of a structured and disciplined approach to the image that your fellowship sends out to your neighbourhood. People respond to professionalism over amateurism: TV property programmes show how the value of a house can go up considerably if some cheap, but effective, cosmetic alterations are carried out. The same principles apply here.

However, don't let producing a corporate identity hinder your work as being a church. People might subconsciously appreciate it, but it is the Gospel message that we want them to respond to.

THREE

TAKE NOTE: NOTICEBOARDS

What will create the first impression about your fellowship? More often than not it's the building; people will look at it, its environment and its noticeboards. It is the exterior of the church – and its signs – that act as a permanent missionary. They suggest whether a church is either dead or alive; if they look tatty they send out negative messages.

A lot of churches have neglected their boards, seeing them as a costly evil, updating them only for a new incumbent. Exposed to the best of British weather, paint peels, rust gathers and wood rots. Hand-painted day-glo posters offering out-of-date service information lies half-torn from hastily pasted boards. And in a few cases, the service information is in that old greasy spoon café lettering, pegged onto a black background and using cApitAl lEtTers in odd places because they've run out of letters. In general, church noticeboards are in a poor state – and this reflects very badly on God's Kingdom.

Hall of shame

Here is a glass fronted church noticeboard from a small country church. Inside the case was a cork-backed board, where there was one note detailing where church key holders live. The rest of the board features large holes in lieu of old notices.

This picture shows a church sign on a large, clear road. Can you spot it? Instead of facing drivers, it's side on. To read it, you have to stop the car.

This sign would be visible if the trees weren't in the way.

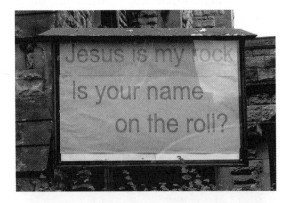

This is a home-made sign, and it shows. The paper is pastel blue, the 'Jesus is my rock' is in a light red text and 'Is your name on the roll?' in green. It's faded and the slogan means nothing: taking the two statements together could make the church sound as if it's taking an 'I'm alright Jack' line. But the slogan relies on people making a jump from rock and roll to get the pun.

This is a clear noticeboard, but the poster on the right lets it down. As it's too small, it becomes a blob surrounded by blank space. Not choosing a poster that fits the space is a schoolboy howler.

This poster has faded and can't be seen from a distance, due to its use of fancy typefaces and complex artwork. There is nothing wrong with this type of poster, but it is only worth using if more people walk past it than drive.

This day-glo poster makes the church look dated through the language such as 'cleanseth us', which means nothing to people who don't realise that their lifestyle is sinful and needs cleansing. The use of paper also doesn't help: never use day-glo paper.

Below is a day-glo poster, half-heartedly ripped down and advertising a spring fair in May. The picture was taken in February, so the sign is at least ten months old. Had there been a Christmas poster, then it would be visible. This is a very poor advert for the church.

This sign is hard to read as it uses gold lettering on an off-white background. There isn't enough contrast between the two elements for it to be clear.

These two signs both come from the same church; they haven't been cleaned up for a long time. Covered with grime, they create the impression that the church is decaying. The slapdash poster advertising its services in the second picture has been thought through: the main services are visible from a distance. However, the weather protection has been done cheaply: it is a 12-part jigsaw puzzle, each piece laminated and then held to the board with drawing pins. To then be placed behind a rotting piece of wood reinforces the make-do image. If the church wanted to create a cheap, but effective and durable sign, they could have bought some vinyl lettering cut to order and stuck it onto a board themselves.

It's very easy to be dismissive of bad church noticeboards, put together on a wing and a prayer, especially when someone has tried their best. But with modern technology making it easier than ever to produce high-quality, low-maintenance and attractive signs, there is little excuse for them. And good church signs do exist. Here are a couple of examples.

This is a board from a Jehovah's Witness meeting hall. The hall is in a cul-de-sac, so this is aimed purely at people passing by on foot. The sign is protected under the church's porch, and is clear and easy to read. It has also been cleaned regularly.

This is a large display board that I designed. It uses vinyl lettering stuck to a large weatherproof board (the main expense) and was produced by a local sign-making company. The church is situated at a major crossroads and the sign is designed to be read by drivers as they wait in traffic jams. On the opposite side of the church's entrance doors is an area for a second sign. This is where we place our own custom made posters, costing about £60 each time.

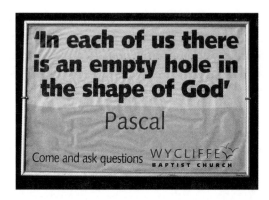

The poster is varied every six weeks and always sticks to the same format: a quote from a well-known person, and the slogan 'come and ask questions' followed by the church's logo. Every day, it is seen by thousands of people, so the poster needs to be memorable. If it was an old-fashioned 'you're going to hell' slogan, it would send out a message that this church judges people before they've even crossed the threshold. The invitation to ask questions shows a willingness to engage in dialogue, something that can then lead to a seeker course.

While you can't beat the professionalism that a computer generated poster brings, talented artists can create stunning posters to display outside your church. Yvonne Coppock from Jersey travels the country offering poster workshops and has written *Prepare the Way with Posters* (Gazelle Books), detailing how to make your own. The key to this ministry is to refresh the posters frequently: 'We change the posters outside the church once a week,' Yvonne says. For more on her ministry, visit www.posterplus.org.uk.

And, for every rule it seems there is an exception. When the Revd Paul Sinclair pastored a London church in the late 80s and early 90s, he created a stunning range of posters that happened to be on day-glo paper. Each one was hand-made, and made ripples in the community. His most famous (below) made it to Sky News.

To create a good poster, he says that simplicity is key. 'A good old fashioned poem, play on words, pun or double entendre

is often best. It helps to be topical, so people can see that you know what's going on in the world.'

Paul's posters worked because they were all unique, tailored to current events, pop culture or the local area. While handmade on a shoestring budget, they were also professionally done and attracted attention because of this. You can see more examples of Paul's former church on his website www.fasterpastor.com.

Work out what you need

A church sign has a shelf life of several years and needs to be easy to update if it lists names or email addresses. Spend money well; there is no point in producing something that will fall apart after a rain shower. Likewise, avoid jargon as it is pointless to produce a sign that could have been written in Martian. What type of church sign do you need? Audit your church grounds, look at the church from the other side of the road, think about who will see the sign and why. Identify groups and rank them into an order: for example, car drivers will see the signs the most as they wait for the lights to change; then people waiting for the bus; then people walking past, etc. Aim the sign at the predominant viewer. If it's motorists, then the amount of text must be reduced to a bare minimum.

The second step is to work out what the sign needs to say. For the first drafts, write out everything you want in full, be it service times, deacons, availability for banns, confessions or drama workshops. Lay this out in a word processing programme, using both portrait and landscape page layouts, to determine which is best. At this stage, don't think about layout, just getting the information on to paper. Seek opinions from people within the church: use this to edit the text down as not a word can be wasted.

Once you have the text agreed, again play around with it using your word processing software. See which layouts work best and which order they need to be – experiment with typefaces as well. Using your corporate identity, choose bold typefaces that can be seen from a distance, and fit in with the image of the church and the sign's immediate surroundings.

Do you want space for posters?

Many churches have space on their noticeboard for a poster – some of the examples show this. Should you buy ready-made ones from catalogues, such as CPO's (www.cpo.org.uk) or make your own? They need changing periodically, especially between Christmas and New Year and just after Easter. There is nothing worse than an out-of-date poster. People are generally forgiving of a poster being left up for a week after the event, but any longer and it makes the church look inactive. Make sure you can buy or make posters that fit the space available.

Get advice from the experts

Visiting sign-making companies is important: obtain several quotes and talk through your ideas with them, letting their experience guide you. Take some photographs of the areas where the church noticeboard will be situated, have some dimensions and some idea of what you want. There are some companies that specialise in church signs, advertising in the Christian press, and there will be some local companies that you can use. A Christian company understands the needs of the church while a local company is a witness opportunity. Don't cut corners on the boards; be prepared to spend several hundred pounds for the initial sign and its installation.

Find out if you need planning permission

Your local authority might need to give planning permission for your sign: in law, noticeboards and crosses are classed as advertisements, like bus shelters and billboards. Consult your district council's planning department for advice. You might also need to apply for permission if your church is a listed building or is in an area of outstanding natural beauty: there is little point in trying to erect a flashing neon sign outside a ninth-century parish church. Making an application will add to your costs, but it's better to do this than hope they turn a blind eye and then pay a hefty legal bill and have to remove them. You will not need planning permission for a sign that is erected inside a building, so if your church has glass-fronted windows, you could erect a sign inside. This will cut costs, but won't stand out.

For more on this, visit the Office of the Deputy Prime Minster's website and read the article 'Outdoor advertisements and signs: a guide for advertisers' (http://www.odpm.gov.uk/index.asp?id=1144634).

What does the sign need to say?

A welcome. The name of the church. The service times. Contact details. Does it need anything else? No, although you might prefer to add the line 'for weddings, christenings and funerals contact ...' If possible, use the church's logo. If you are an Anglican church, you don't need to list which parish you belong too.

For example:

Collinstone Community Church

Bringing the community together

We welcome you to
Collinstone Community Church
Services every Sunday, 10.30 a.m. & 6.30 p.m.
Tel: 567890 Email: office@ccchurch.co.uk
Web: www.ccchurch.co.uk

Note that the example above doesn't include the name of the church pastor. Using the email address is enough. However, if you feel you have to include the name of the church leader, you can safely ditch the qualifications and use their Christian name instead. So don't have the Revd Dr Hartnell BD, BSc, MA, etc: just the Revd Dr Christopher Hartnell is enough.

Don't use language that is archaic: do people know what you mean when you say matins or the Lord's Supper? There is also no need to mention the church's other activities. You might want to add a line 'Other activities during the week, contact office for details' and have a leaflet, a website or an email ready for any enquirers. Alternatively, you could have a smaller sign somewhere close by listing these meetings. Some parish churches list these in the porch; other churches will have a board set up inside a glass-fronted entrance door. Another suggestion is to have a scrolling LED-display sign listing these groups – ideal if you are by a bus stop and have a captive audience.

Keep the board in sympathy with the surroundings

The board must be designed to reflect the immediate area. If the church was built in the 1980s, then creating a wooden board with gothic script lettering and carved cherubs would be out of step. Choose colours, materials and typefaces carefully. Everything should gel together to create one aesthetically pleasing environment.

Don't forget the elements and vandals

The experience of the sign makers will come into its own here. They should be able to advise you on the best materials to use to avoid letting your board become the victim of either the elements or vandals. Consider fixing the signs to the front of the church, out of reach of any would-be vandal. There is little you can do about the weather, but be sure to continue to apply waterproofing materials and keep the board clean. Find out from the sign maker which cleaning materials to use and write a cleaning date into the church diary. Remember that a dirty sign reflects badly on the church itself.

Don't be cheap

Spending as little as possible to create a board that won't stand up to the elements, or look tacky, even from a distance, is wasted money. It's better to produce a good board once and maintain it over its lifetime.

If you want to create your own posters

I've got a collection of terrible church slogans. These are the cheesy posters that inspired the book and do the Church

no favours. Think of 'Free Trip to heaven. Details Inside!';
'Fight truth decay – study the Bible daily'; 'Dusty Bibles lead
to Dirty Lives'. You must have your favourites. They might be
witty to believers, but think about them: what do they say to
people who have no idea how the Bible could be relevant to
their lives? Nothing. They do not witness effectively. What is
'truth decay'? The church is judging someone by suggesting
they're dirty for not opening a Bible. The stench of cheese
from 'CH__CH, what's missing? UR' is nauseating. There is
nothing to commend these slogans or others like them. Ditch
them and the day-glo paper that they rest on.

As discussed for logos, avoid using biblical quotes, especially
those written in old English; no one speaks it, and Jesus
certainly didn't. 'Posters for Churches', an anonymous article
on the Free Presbyterian Church of Scotland website and
published November 2005, takes the opposite view:

> *Appropriate posters are those which have verses from Scripture, such
> as: "Seek ye the Lord while He may be found" … These verses carry
> God's authority with them. They speak to sinners' deepest needs, and
> we may expect God to bless them.*

The problem with having posters with verses on is that they
will not be understood by non-churchgoers. They do not speak
to people in the same way that a contemporary poster aimed at
your neighbourhood will. So, if your church is in an area where
a large youth population hang around, produce something
aimed at them. We want to get people into church, and given
that people think the Bible is boring, we first have to reach
out to their level to draw them inside. On this basis, we should
choose Bible verses that will inspire and encourage rather than
judge and condemn. Alternatively, look for different ways of
expressing our faith through the poster: perhaps a picture of

someone from the fellowship with a one-sentence testimony: 'Jesus cured my insecurity'; 'Ask me how I know the Bible is true'. Using personal stories that people can relate to will be more effective than a verse from a book that they have vague ideas about.

The idea that my church uses is quotes from celebrities about God e.g. 'I'm approaching the end of my life. There's a sense of not being fulfilled, and it bothers me' William Shatner (Captain Kirk) and 'People are dying inside, marriage problems, financial problems, drug problems, and they don't know how to escape. My life was changed through Jesus' Nigel Benn, world boxing champion. How are they found? One idea is to look out for interviews with the stars and quote from them. The concept taps into people's fascination with all things celebrity. If you're in any doubt about what to put on the posters, pray and deliberate in a group.

Could you use handmade posters?

Yes; but they have to be executed to a very high standard. Be critical about the posters produced. Don't waste time or resources producing a poor-quality, second-rate effort that will give a bad impression. The key to this ministry is to keep it fresh. There is little point in producing say, four hand-made posters and then rotating them. The elements will quickly spoil the artwork – wet weather will make them damp, bright sunshine will cause fading. People will remember the old posters and realise quite quickly that the church hasn't blessed this ministry with the necessary financial resources.

Computer generated

Computers have transformed the entire sign industry, and it is possible to create high-quality full-colour posters using your own home computer. There are a range of printing firms who offer large-scale print outs – the *Yellow Pages* will be able to point you in the right direction. Before approaching them, have a list of requirements:

- The size of the board in millimetres.
- What type of board – does it have a Perspex cover or is the poster exposed to the elements? This will determine whether you need weatherproof inks or normal ones.
- How often you will change the posters over the course of a year? Every month? Six weeks?
- How graphical do you want to make them? Just text or do you want to include images?
- What software have you got on your computer?
- If it's not compatible, or you don't have the skill, how much would the firm charge to produce the artwork?

Talk to a few firms and invite them to quote for a year's contract – find out if they will offer a discount if you set up one poster to use as an artwork template and change the text each time. They might offer a discount if they know that you will give regular business. When are they likely to be busy? There is no point in giving them a poster and demanding an instant turnaround when they're trying to meet a deadline for a large multinational company.

Setting the tone for your church through its noticeboards and signs is one of the hardest aspects of the church's publicity; it's worth getting it right.

FOUR

CATHEDRAL TO CHAPEL: THE CHURCH BUILDING

I f a church's exterior noticeboards are on permanent publicity duties (always witnessing just by being there) then how important is the rest of the church's environment? The buildings themselves are just as much part of the publicity as printed items. In this chapter we'll look at some of the areas which deserve attention, much of which should come under basic maintenance of your church's property, regardless of whether your church buildings are centuries old, a tin-tabernacle or a recently built warehouse-type complex. Use these tips as a starting point and remember your church building is a permanent advert for the Kingdom.

The church grounds

The environment that the church stands in is important. From a building nestled in a chocolate-box scene to one that's in the middle of a housing estate, our churches have to be God's lighthouses. If the very ground that the church stands in is left to decay, the chances are people will think that the church is likewise in decline. By spending time looking after the immediate vicinity of the church, you will help change the way people perceive and relate to it. The danger is in going too far and turning the church into a National Trust garden: are you more concerned with looking after the building than people?

Litter picking

Picking up litter is like shovelling snow in a blizzard, but it has to be done. The church grounds can often be a dumping ground for all kinds of rubbish and there could be needles, so take care. In the Channel 4 programme *Priest Idol*, it was appalling to watch the vicar of Lundwood's parish church waste his ministry time by cleaning up the church's grounds regularly. Find volunteers in the fellowship that can do this on a weekly or daily basis.

Graffiti and vandalism

It's a frustrating and costly nuisance, but also a fact of life. Do what you can to minimise the risk; erect some CCTV (dummy or real) if need be. I hate seeing churches that have wire grills, bolted doors and barbed wire as it suggests that the church is under constant attack. Instead, invite your community police officer to walk round the site and offer practical crime prevention suggestions. Contact the local council and see what services they provide for removing graffiti. But don't leave it: it's an invitation to others. The London Borough of Richmond offers some guidelines for helping prevent graffiti build-up. These include:

- Avoid the use of extremes of light and dark colour on external wall and door finishes.
- Use non-porous or impermeable surface treatments (e.g. tiles) on external walls and doors.
- Provide good external lighting but in accordance with planning guidelines.
- Use railings rather than solid fencing on property boundaries.
- Grow climbing plants on suitable external walls and fences.
- Report all graffiti to the police as it is criminal damage – they will use the information to help fight crime. (http://www.richmond.gov.uk/graffiti_pledge.pdf)

Maintain the church grounds

The *Priest Idol* series also revealed beautiful church grounds: a large grassy area ideal for summer parties, a small children's playground and a garden area where plants could be grown. When the new priest arrived, these areas were neglected and overgrown, reinforcing the myth that the Church is dying. When they were transformed by landscape gardeners, the difference was incredible, and the space is usable. Many people in your fellowship will be green-fingered – ask them to get involved by creating an appropriate garden for your neighbourhood. It might be one of the few green spaces in your area, so think about whether to include benches and bins for people to use. Don't be afraid to fence the area off and lock it at night; no one can smell flowers in the dark.

Maintain the car park

Look out for potholes, markings that are fading, signs that are coming down. The area should be well-lit for night time gatherings, and so that people will feel safe while walking from their car to the church doors. Ensure that any bike racks are secure, and a steward is patrolling the car park during services to deter thieves.

Car parking

This is common sense: don't let people park their cars badly. Flip the 'what would Jesus drive' slogan around to get: 'how would Jesus park?' The answer would no doubt be with consideration for other motorists – and pedestrians. A few years ago, members of one local church took to parking their cars on the pavement outside, rather than make arrangements to use a car park across the road. People with pushchairs said they couldn't get past the parked cars and the mess gave the church some very bad publicity. We have to ensure our parking is an advert for the Kingdom. Park legally, don't take spaces away from local residents, don't block the road and be willing to move your car if asked. The best way to avoid all this is to walk to church.

Paint

One of the quickest ways to let a church look rundown is if the paintwork is peeling. It's a major job, but it's worth doing as it creates a good impression.

Interior signs and noticeboards

The interior signs are just as important as the exterior ones. Not every visitor will stop and read each rota, but the chances are they will look at the board featuring pictures of the church leadership team. It's important to keep the house in order, and this section will give some suggestions for this.

Signposting

Churches are unique buildings, each one built and expanded upon over centuries, or purpose built for the twenty-first century. Full of nooks and crannies, it can be hard for a visitor to navigate their way to the toilets, especially when they are hidden away. One church's toilets are next to its private offices: could visitors spend a penny without wondering if anyone would think that their intentions were less than pure? Signposts are very helpful things, and can easily be created using a computer and good quality printer. This is where your corporate identity comes in.

- Think carefully about what directional signs are needed in your church building: church hall, toilets, crèche, quiet room, prayer room, cloakroom and so on.

- Work out which of these is the longest: this will determine the size of lettering on your sign. You can use a word processing package, but desk top publishing software will let you adjust the spacing between letters (the kerning), this will let you fit more letters into a line:

Unkerned text
kerned text

- Set your page as A4 landscape. Using these settings, you can create two lines, and two signs. Use a strong, dark colour (black is fine, but your church's colour might be purple) for the lettering, or have the lettering as white text on a dark background. Remember these signs have to be legible from a distance, so keep the text large, visible and use a bold typeface. Test them before creating a whole series.

- Print these out onto a good quality sheet of white paper (it doesn't have to be photoglossy paper, but some thin 160gsm card could be useful).

- Using spray mount (glue sold in aerosol cans and found in craft shops) attach the sheet of paper to a piece of foam board (also from a craft shop). Foam board is a lightweight material used in exhibition design and can easily be cut with a sharp craft knife and a metal ruler. It can be bought in any size from A5 up to A0: in this example, use A4. Do not use other forms of glue: spray mount will hold all the corners of the paper in place. Follow the instructions on the can, it's best sprayed outside.

- Using a craft knife and a metal ruler, cut the foam board so you have two pieces of paper both 297mm in width and 105mm high. Your signs are now ready to be installed in the church. With some Velcro on the back, they will attach themselves to fabric boards, with string attached into them they can be hung from the ceiling (and will blow in a breeze). They can also be glued into position.

- You might consider protecting the sign by covering it with sticky back plastic. It takes the patience of a saint to avoid bubbles when applying and it might create a glare when light shines on it. Only use if you're sure it will be a help rather than a hindrance.

- If you wanted to make larger signs, such as an A3 one, you could print out the signs and enlarge them with a colour photocopier, or take the artwork to a print shop and ask them to output the signs from your disk.

These are not permanent signs: sometimes the spray mount will dry out and foam board dents easily if dropped. However, they are a budget way of producing good quality signs and are useful as a short term solution.

If you want proper signs, then talk to a local signmaker. Go along with photographs of where you want the signs to go and how large you want them. They will be able to produce high quality work that will last for several years. The vinyl cut lettering can be removed should the signs need to be updated.

The noticeboards

There are two pet hates for noticeboards: boards that are falling apart and notices that are out of date. Money can be an issue for many churches, which is why old boards are left to decay. There are some cost-effective solutions: cork tiles can be pasted onto a wall and replaced every couple of years. Someone in the fellowship with DIY skills can create felt-covered boards, but it's worth obtaining quotes from sign makers. It might be better to install some metallic boards and hold notices in place with magnets. The ideal solution will vary from church to church, so be imaginative and creative: but keep it smart.

A church noticeboard needs notices. These can be all small ads (house shares, for sale, etc.), news of missionaries, forthcoming events and events taking place within the fellowship. An incredible amount of work is going on in God's Kingdom: that means a lot of publicity materials are being produced and placed on notices. After the event, or when the house share has been let, why don't the people who placed the posters take them down again? Time and again, notices are left languishing on boards, unloved and unneeded, so someone needs to police the boards. If notices are dated, they can be checked in time for the forthcoming Sunday and anything that shouldn't be there can be removed. The boards are then a useful resource.

There's also a problem with drawing pins: there's either too many or not enough. How many times have you noticed a notice hanging loosely because they've not been pinned properly? If there is an overseer for the boards, then this will be less of a problem. The overseer will also be able to position notices neatly, making the boards look more professional. It sounds like officialdom gone mad, but it will really help churches appear to be more professional.

It's worth putting everything into clear sections, perhaps roped off with some ribbon – what's on, for sale, church events, youth events, etc. Create some suitable headings in the same house style as the church signs. Simple touches like this will help the user find what they're interested in and make it easier to manage the boards.

If you have pictures of the church leadership team, ensure they are up to date

Taking pictures used to be a chore: developing was expensive, the quality and poses varied and there was no way of knowing whether heads had been chopped off until the prints came back. Now thanks to digital cameras, all this has changed: uniform pictures can easily and quickly be taken, they can be checked for quality and can be cropped so that they are all the same size and style. Get the church leadership team together on the same day, at the same time once a year. Do this at the same point in time every year and update the pictures annually. For full details on taking mugshots, see chapter 16.

The alternative, which depends very much on the type of church you are, is to encourage the church leaders to submit pictures of them taking part in a leisure activity, be it a hobby, holiday or funny moment. The downside to this is that it could be harder for people to identify the church leaders: candid snapshots don't always look like the person does in real life.

Make sure that it's clear who is who in each picture; it's harder for people to identify an uncaptioned photo, especially if there are several people in it and only one of them is, say, the church's deacon.

Banners

Banners adorn the walls of many of our churches, often tableaux designed to help us meditate on Scripture. It appears that they have evolved from banners created to identify churches and Sunday school groups; similar to the way in which old trade unions had their own banners used for when they went on marches and rallies. (For more on this, log on to: www.bbc.co.uk/history/society_culture/protest_reform/banners_01.shtml).

Banner-making groups are still meeting in many churches, often producing beautiful pieces. But some banners look like they've been thrown together using 1970s material. The quality of the banners that are hung in churches is indicative of the church's general attitude: it might not be a conscious decision, but if the church is happy to display mediocre banners, then the chances are that this attitude of make-do will prevail elsewhere. It does no one any favours: banners are an offering to God, in time, in creativity and God-given gifts. One only has to look to the temple built by Solomon to realise how important the décor of the temple was to the Israelites. This is the attitude we need with our church banners; someone in the church leadership team should be willing to vet them at an early stage to ensure that time, energy and materials are not being wasted.

Dusting

It hardly needs to be said, but a dusty church looks like a building that hasn't been used much. If you have people coming in for a Christening, a wedding or a funeral, you can change their impression of the Church if there's no dust for them to see! Dusting, cleaning and polishing is a thankless task, often left to volunteers or the caretaker. Organise cleaning parties and make the chore fun. Remember that it's the attitude we have towards our buildings that is the publicity agent here: showing respect suggests that we care about them, leaving them dirty suggests that we don't.

Taking care of our church buildings really will help them stand out; ensuring they sparkle means they will be seen as the lighthouses that our communities desperately need.

FIVE

LOVING SUNDAY:
MAKING THE MOST OF THE
SUNDAY EXPERIENCE

What do non-Christians think about the church experience? Some friends gave me the following comments: 'I always avoided going to church ... simply because the services are boring and uncomfortable.' 'It's a bit dull, in the same way that *Pebble Mill* [a lunchtime chat show] used to be a bit dull.' The reason for this? Some churches are a vision of hell on earth rather than heaven.

It's not just non-Christians that endure bad services; I arrived early for one speaking engagement, hoping for a cuppa, an order of service and a lunch invite. No one welcomed me or asked if I was a visitor. At the post-church coffee time, I waited in vain for someone to come and talk to me. The church huddled around the edges, making me feel conspicuous; one can only imagine that everyone was wrapped up in discussing that morning's sermon. Despite broad hints about lunch, the morning ended with me waving the minister goodbye as he drove off. Needless to say, I'm in no rush to go back, and I know their attitude to visitors is replicated in other churches. Over this chapter, we're going to look at the whole church experience and work out how we can make it more user-friendly for guests.

Everyone in the fellowship must play their part

Do you remember sandwich boards: people walking up and down high streets wearing boards bearing slogans such as 'Eat at Joe's Café'? Well, that's what you are like as a Christian. Everything we say and do to visitors of a church makes us a walking advert for the Gospel and we would do well to remember this. Rick Warren's *The Purpose Driven Church* makes this point: 'Long before the pastor preaches, the visitors are already deciding whether or not they will come back. They are asking themselves, "Do I feel welcome here?"' The onus is not on the church's pastors to be welcoming, but on everyone a visitor comes into contact with. We need to think of a Sunday service as an experience where people decide they belong according to the welcome, communication, environment, audibility, visibility, music style and quality, worship sensitivity, sense of God's presence, sense of a caring community, clean toilets, quality of coffee and chat. If we take all these seriously, visitors will want to belong.

Welcoming people

For visitors, merely entering the building is a huge step. They might be nervous, shy or wondering what they're doing. Newcomers won't know anything: they need reassurance, guidance and a friendly face that will make them feel welcome, wanted and worthy. So why do the people who stand on church doors avoid eye contact, mumble and offer a very half-hearted handshake? This is a first impression – and it matters as it sets the tone for the whole worship experience.

Treat people how you want to be treated. Carry out a simple audit on the church: without warning the greeters, get someone, preferably a non-Christian or non-regular attendee, to road-test the welcome. Look out for the things that visitors will want to know on arrival – are they greeted with a smile and a firm handshake? Do the greeters look the visitor in the eye and offer a word of welcome? When people go through the doors into the church sanctuary is someone on hand to offer hymn-books, notice sheets and another welcome? Is it obvious that those stewards are there to help during the service? Is the service sheet self-explanatory, or will the order of the relevant sections of the service book be explained from the front? If there is a crèche or children's activities, will your visitors be able to find out about it before the service starts?

There are a lot of questions to think of here, but they must be asked because we need to ensure that the church is a welcoming and positive environment where people are able to be themselves. If they come into a building where they're scowled at and left to their own devices, will they then feel quite so free to worship God, or will they have one eye on the door to leave as soon as the service ends?

The Revd Dr Alistair Brown, general director of BMS World Mission, once pastored a church in Aberdeen. He told me: 'On very cold winter days – sometimes snow was falling – the stewards would open only one part of the large double doors. Worshippers crept round and disappeared into an unseen interior. It looked like we were a secret society creeping in for secret ceremonies. Not at all welcoming. No one in the neighbourhood struggling with the decision whether or not to brave church for the first time would ever have dared enter. So I told the stewards we had to open the doors wide and look like we were in business. They protested that it was too cold. I said we had to do it anyway, and to put a heavier coat on if necessary. To their credit they did and, being a thoughtful and kind church, we soon also installed some warm heaters above the entrance doors which were pointed in the direction of those waiting to greet attendees. The side benefit, I reckon, was that the red of the heaters gave them an angelic glow. All were happy. Numbers grew, no doubt for more reasons than merely opening the doors properly, but a church which doesn't look like it wants "strangers" will find it never gets them.'

Good handshakes

It's important to give a good handshake, but be careful to get this right. A weak handshake, where little physical contact is made, is an almost apologetic welcome. At the same time, shaking someone's arm off will give the impression that you are arrogant and overbearing. If you have the privilege of welcoming people into your church, practise your handshake: be firm, look someone in the eye and smile.

Words of welcome

As you shake hands, you should offer some words of welcome. You might feel self-conscious but try not to – you are the host greeting these strangers. The best solution, especially when you have a queue, is to rotate a series of stock phrases. Be sincere, people will react to your tone. Here are my opening phrases:

- 'Good morning, it's lovely to see to you'
- 'A very warm welcome to you'
- 'Thank you for joining us today'
- 'Hello, thanks for coming'
- 'Welcome, hope you enjoy worshipping with us today'
- 'It's great to see you. Thanks for joining us'

If it's someone I know well, I'm not afraid to hold their arm with my other hand when shaking their hand, give a hug or a kiss on the cheek if appropriate. This is based on Paul's command to greet one another with a holy kiss. Obviously certain caveats apply: I only welcome people in this way if the friendship is solid enough and it is culturally acceptable to do so. I never kiss children, but shake their hand; they are the church of today and deserve to be welcomed as such. Often, they are too shy to accept the hand of a stranger, but you should make the effort.

As long as there is someone on the door offering a kind word of welcome, there can be no excuse for any visitor to say that no one spoke to them when they came to your church. For the visitor, the type of welcome will set the scene for the rest of their visit, so regard this as a ministry and get it right.

'Welcoming' on the way out

These principles also apply to people on the way out: be friendly, look people in the eye and thank them for coming. If the church offers refreshments, point people in the direction of the hall. If they have to leave, then you can always say, 'Have a good week, look forward to seeing you again soon.'

Inside the building, where next?

Now people have been welcomed, they will need to know where to go. This might sound obvious but what if the visitor needs the toilet? Or it's their first time in any church and need some guidance? You'll also need to consider the building's signage: would it help to have directions to the hall, the toilets and the sanctuary? Is there a welcome desk where visitors can collect information about the fellowship?

If your church has the luxury of people, then have some welcoming on the doors, some handing out hymn-books and a front-of-house person – a main point of contact standing in the no-man's-land between the entrance and the sanctuary. If you have two ministers in the church, then the one who is not preaching could take on this role, as guests will be made to feel more welcome if a member of the pastoral staff is there. The main role of the front-of-house staff is to answer any questions that the visitor has and to befriend them by finding out a bit about them: hence the suggestion of involving the pastors. However, it can be undertaken by anyone who is comfortable talking to strangers and knows their way around the church, not just the geography but who the various people are, with their hobbies and interests. If this is known then after the service appropriate introductions can be made, e.g. teachers with teachers, musicians with musicians. Consider making badges for volunteer stewards and pastoral staff to wear.

Stewards

When people go into the sanctuary, they will usually be given another greeting from the people who hand out hymn-books and service sheets. This is often done with robotic efficiency: hand out the book and onto the next person. In other churches, there's a nervous fumble as the volunteer brings together the service sheet with service books, rarely looking up. And in newer churches, where everything is projected onto the big screen, there's no one offering anything, not even a box of popcorn. This generalisation neglects the many churches where the volunteers are only too happy to help; giving books with a smile, showing people where they can sit (useful if there is a designated parent and toddler area or a parade service on and seats are reserved). These people generally come early to sort out the books and service sheets so that they are ready. They are pleased to offer a smile and they help reinforce good impressions. Remember, we don't want people saying that no one talked to them, or that the church wasn't friendly.

Stewards shouldn't tell people that they can't sit there because Mrs Jones always sits there – if Mrs Jones isn't already there then that's her problem. Some friends of a pastor visited a country church and went to sit in an empty pew. They were ordered out because, once a year, the lady of the nearby manor attends church services and sits in that pew: she was not in church that Sunday. How rude to then ask their guests to move!

Stewards should also be briefed on issues that will affect disabled people: large print hymn-books and service sheets should be available; the sound desk should have prepared a map showing the 'black spots' of the hearing aid loop and there should be spaces for wheelchairs. Stewards should sensitively offer this information to anyone who needs it. This should not be a burden, although it forms part of the requirements of the Disability Discrimination Act of 2005 (for more, see: http://www.direct.gov.uk/DisabledPeople) we have a moral obligation to make church (a meeting place of all God's people) accessible to all. Those leading worship should point out that stewards are available to assist people during the entire service.

The start of the service

Usually a service starts with a welcome from the front. Introduce yourself to people, putting yourself into context: instead of 'welcome to Collinstone Community Church', say, 'Hello, my name is Phil, I'm one of the pastors here, and I'd like to welcome you today as we worship God together.' This preamble should also help answer questions that visitors will have. Is there a crèche? Are refreshments available? Where are the toilets? Can I keep my mobile on? Obviously how much detail you go into depends on the type of service. Look out for the visitors in the congregation and tailor information accordingly.

Ditch the jargon

'One of the problems with the spindly types then used by newspapers was partly the fault of the dry-molding of stereotypes, which required heavier pressures than the obsolescent wet matrix process.'

So says Alexander Lawson in *Anatomy of a Typeface*. Have you got any idea what that means? If not, then what hope have non-churchgoers got when you start spouting away with religious jargon? This is not an appeal for church leaders to start producing dumbed-down sermons but people will not always understand what you mean, especially if they are not Christians. It's always worth explaining the Gospel in every sermon, be it in the sermon or through a testimony.

Think about other bits of jargon that might need explaining: what measuring unit is a cubit? Jesus used parables that spoke in the language and customs of the time, so it's only natural that they need to be unpacked for today's world.

Likewise, there are other bits of jargon to avoid. Take this notice: 'If you want to go on the Futures away day, see Mary', it means nothing. Try: 'Teenagers are invited to join the Futures away day. The youth group is going bowling and if you want more details see Mary Jones' – and invite her to stand up. Keep making things clear. Keep explaining yourself.

Following the order of service

Does your church use the *Book of Common Prayer and Common Worship*? Perhaps you use Psalms for responsive readings. Sometimes, the combination of the books, the hymn-books and the service sheet means you need more arms than an octopus to keep tabs on the liturgy. For a visitor, it's terribly confusing, especially if there are instructions such as, 'The minister may use a seasonal sentence before using one or more of the penitential sentences.' If there's no explanation from the front of the church you can get stuck in an endless round of catch-up. The answer is to buy an electronic version of the texts from Church House Publishing and produce a tailor-made order of service in a word processing or desktop publishing programme. This ensures that everyone knows what's coming next and will be able to participate fully. Ensure that you include guidelines about when people need to stand, sit or kneel; if you're a church that encourages people to talk before the service starts, then make it clear when people need to quieten down – perhaps a signal such as a cross being illuminated or the choir entering.

The notices

It's a long-running joke that the notices can go on and on – there have been services where the announcements were longer than the sermon. It's unnecessary and tedious. Think about what needs to be said in the service, especially if you have a notice sheet. As a rule of thumb, don't give out a notice if there's a mention in the notice sheet; instead point members of the congregation in its direction.

The collection

If you've ever been church hopping, you'll know that the subtleties of different services can take you by surprise; this is apparent during the time set aside for the collection. How churches choose to take people's monetary gifts varies. Unless anyone explains what's about to happen, your guests are going to be left in the dark. It's easy to feel foolish if you don't know that when the collection is brought to the front, everyone stands. The worship leader needs to explain what will happen. Remember that people perceive the Church as money-grabbing, rich and over-funded. So, it's easy to say, 'We're about to take the collection for Collinstone Community Church. It's a free-will offering and there's no need for guests or visitors to give. A lot of people give through their bank accounts, and therefore pass the plate without putting anything into it – you won't be the only one not giving.'

And ensure that people know what's happening. For example, 'The stewards will pass the plates around, when they've finished they'll walk to the front and we'll all stand and give thanks.'

Do you need to take a collection? If most of the congregation give by direct debit could you have wall-mounted collection boxes so people can give on the way out? Don't let it be authoritarian, and don't let people think they have to pay to pray.

Communion

Some churches have strict rules about who can or can't take the bread and wine, others have their quirks. In many Free Churches, anyone who has made a commitment can take communion. The congregation is served in the pews, where they eat the bread as it's received but drink the wine together as a symbol of our unity. It's also common to go up to the priest and receive communion in turn, but how do you indicate that you don't want to take part?

It will add about thirty seconds to your service to explain exactly what will happen. You can do it quite simply by saying something like this: 'Collinstone Community Church is about to celebrate communion, a meal that Jesus instructed us to do in memory of him. In our church, if you are a believer, then we are happy for you to take communion. We will have a short prayer and then people will bring bread and wine round. Eat the bread when you receive it and use the silence to pray and focus on what Jesus did on the cross. When you receive the wine – non-alcoholic grape juice – hold on to your cup, and we'll all drink together. The empty cups will be collected by the stewards during the final hymn.'

Similarly, if you encourage people to go up to the priest to receive communion, then ensure that the stewards are ready to tell people when to go up. There's nothing worse than wondering when to go up – and having people tutting because you don't know what to do.

If there's a collection after the communion, make it clear where the money will go to, and that it is a voluntary offering. Don't let people leave the building thinking they have to pay twice for the privilege of being in God's house.

Prayer after the service

Some visitors come to church because they face a crisis in their lives. They'll sit patiently through a service because they want to turn to God in their moment of need. Empathise with them: they're in your church because they're seeking help. After an hour of worship with no friendly faces welcoming them, they can leave feeling no one seems to care about their burdens.

Can your fellowship offer an area for prayer and listening after the service? It doesn't need the minister – just people who are confident in listening and then praying for the person in front of them. Situations might arise when the pastor or elders might need to intervene, but most people will be glad to have someone to pray with. The easiest way to start praying for people is to have the prayer team come to the front during the final hymn, wearing identifying badges. The person leading the service could say a bit like this: 'If you want prayer for something, then don't leave here without getting help. Straight after the service, some volunteers will be here [point at the area] waiting to pray with you. We know that God hears our prayers and answers them – don't leave with a burden to carry by yourself.'

The three-minute rule

Talking to people after a church service is one of the many reasons why people will come back to churches: they enjoy the fellowship. We naturally seek out people who we feel comfortable with, so it's understandable that as soon as the service finishes, people talk to their friends instead of focusing on the stranger in their midst. My common experience is that if I want to meet with the people in the church I'm visiting, then it's up to me. This approach requires people to be comfortable in talking to strangers, but the onus should be on the home side to make the visitors feel welcome.

The easiest route is to have people in the fellowship who are happy to approach strangers to talk to them. This merely requires the church to identify them and give them this ministry. The medium route, which is less risky but might upset those who see the service as sacrosanct, is to invite people to talk to their neighbours during the collection. This works because it's for a limited time period and is led from the front.

However, the hardest route is also the most rewarding, especially if you have a large church and don't know everyone. It's the three-minute rule, as suggested by Rick Warren in his book *The Purpose Driven Church* and the churches that practice it will soon find people getting to know one another much faster. The rule is simple: for the first three minutes after the service, those present should try and talk to people that they don't know. Conversations can be continued with a post-service cuppa: often superficial chit-chat about the weather, the football and the weather (again). Here's a typical conversational exchange:

> PERSON A – 'Hi. How are you?'
> PERSON B – 'Fine thanks. How you are?'
> PERSON A – 'Fine. Bit cold today isn't it?'
> PERSON B – 'Yes, I've had to wrap up warm.'
> PERSON A – 'Oh. OK. Nice to see you. Bye.'

This reads terribly but it really does happen; our typical 'British reserve' means that church members struggle to open up to strangers. We can easily make our churches more welcoming if we're willing to ask questions that provoke more of a response. When interviewing someone, journalists will rarely ask questions that invite a yes or no answer. So, instead of asking 'do you like roast beef?' you can turn the question slightly: 'What is your favourite meal?' And if people say 'roast beef' you can then ask them why. Instead of being an exchange of facts, it's a conversation of feelings. It's warmer and more intimate, because it involves opening up to someone.

Lunch and fellowship

One of the most generous ministries that anyone can exhibit is inviting strangers back into their homes for a meal. It's also a biblical command: in Romans 12:13, Paul simply says 'Practise hospitality'. It costs very little to add a few extra potatoes to the pot, make up some extra gravy and set an extra place at the dining table. However, some people might feel uncomfortable in inviting a stranger round. Some might want to invite, but feel that their home is too small, too messy or that they can't cook. That's fine – don't feel guilty about gifts or circumstances that you don't have. However, it's no excuse for spending time with our brothers and sisters in fellowship. You could find a pub close to the church that offers Sunday lunches: a group can easily go along and enjoy a meal and each others' company. The beauty of a pub meal is that people can choose according to their budget or time. Some might come along for a short time; others might stay and watch the football. As you're a group of Christians, there should be little pressure to drink alcohol and no one should feel awkward just having a soft drink. Even if some people won't go because it's a Sunday, because it's a pub or that they don't like the food, at least you've made an invitation that will make them feel valued.

An alternative to offering food or instant fellowship straight after the service is to ask if they want to meet for a coffee during the week. If we really want to exercise a ministry that welcomes people and helps them think of the Church as a caring community, then real fellowship is vital. Spending time listening and talking to one another is important and should not be undervalued. If all of this feels beyond you, then talk about this as a fellowship. There are usually a few people who are happy to invite people round, and may be willing to set up a rota so that they don't feel burdened every Sunday. That's not to say that your visitors won't have made plans of their own, but the offer is just as important. Which church will you think of more highly: the one where you always receive a lunch invite or the one where the warden rattles keys to kick people out?

SIX

GETTING TECHNICAL:
USING OHPs, TVs AND POWERPOINT

Do you still use hymn-books? Increasingly, churches are ditching the books and relying on both overhead projectors (OHPs) or using TV monitors hooked up to a computer. The big advantage is that people are able to worship God freely: they can wave their hands in the air, clap or even keep them in their pockets. There are other benefits: services can be tailor-made, taking into account the readings, hymns and songs from a variety of different sources and it can offer a visual aid to ministers wanting to help people remember parts of the sermon. The disadvantages include the problem of power cuts, computer theft or malfunction – all drastic. More commonly, people haven't thought through how the slides will be used in the church, making them illegible to all but the most eagle-eyed. The best advice you can get on setting up your church for PowerPoint or other similar software packages, is to read Jackie Sheppard's *Beyond The*

OHP, a user-friendly book that will help determine what your church needs.

One church I visited gave me a complete master class in how not to use PowerPoint (or OHP slides), including just about everything to avoid in just one sermon. A lot of their mistakes will appear over the coming pages, but the only reason that I was able to spot them is because I too had once succumbed to the temptations of an all-singing, all-dancing presentation. Instead of using PowerPoint as a tool, I became its slave and, as the presentation wore on, my audience could have learnt everything from the slides. Similarly, had the computer not worked, my presentation would have been sunk, as my script relied on being able to talk through the slides. Plan what you want to say, and use only keywords on the PowerPoint or OHP slide – watch how television news bulletins use graphics to make an emphasis during reports; the slides complement rather than detract from the reporter. For example, if you're giving a sermon on the nature of the cross, then you might say this: 'Christ suffered from the moment he was sentenced to the moment he died. He was whipped and flogged by his captors. They mocked him and chose to divide his clothes up by casting lots. Then he was forced to carry his heavy wooden cross to Calvary – a journey which is hard enough when you're dragging a large piece of wood along the ground, but near impossible when you've already endured suffering and pain. When he arrived at Calvary, long nails were driven through his wrists and feet, holding him to the cross. He was then suspended in such a way that to breathe, he had to drag himself up, take a breath and then go down again. It was suffering beyond anything we can ever imagine. And he did that because he loved us.'

The slide can simply be: 'Christ was forced to suffer before he died'. This short summary helps the listener focus on the sermon.

In my church, the computer operators went through a phase of having a keyword underneath a picture of the preacher, changing it when appropriate. A great idea, but it was let down when they came to the word 'anti-Christ' – for a few minutes, my pastor was called the enemy.

By far the most common problem with using PowerPoint, or similar presentation management systems, is the child in a sweetshop syndrome. The programmes are powerful, offering features that are useful but not terribly practical. For example, lines of text can be made to appear on the screen as and when needed and at the touch of a button. The best way for the church audience is also the simplest: just let it appear with no snap, crackle or pop. However tempting, don't take the focus away from your sermon by letting the letters bounce in as if taking part in a *Come Dancing* contest. And don't let them be stretched, squashed, squeezed or any of the other fancy effects you can choose. The reason is simple: people come to church to hear the Word of God expounded upon, they should not be distracted by opportunities that the church itself has provided. If people come away from the service remembering the fancy graphics and nothing of the actual message then you have failed.

This is also true of sound clips. The preacher mentioned earlier had put a lot of thought and care into his presentation and managed to find a picture of a police car with a sound clip of a siren to illustrate his point that there are times when you don't want to see the police, such as when you're speeding. The parallel point in his sermon was that there are times when you don't want to see God because those are times when you are sinning. It was a good illustration, but ruined by continuing to play the siren long after he had moved on to the next point. Eventually, he had to ask the sound operator to turn it off – but he really shouldn't have had to. Using the sound clip was a good idea as it reinforced the point he was making, but he was wrong not to decide how long the siren should have been heard for. If you're going to use special effects, plan them well in advance, ensure that they are there to complement rather that detract from your message. You will also need to ensure that the sound desk knows when to fade the sound in and out.

The other problem with the images that this pastor chose was that they were American and obviously so. While most people will forgive seeing an American police car, they would be less forgiving of being asked to make a choice of following God when the illustration is of a man flanked by a Republican Elephant and a Democrat Donkey, hunched over his shoulders as if they were a devil and an angel. In the sermon in question, they were animated, moving back and forth for several minutes, causing an unnecessary diversion just as the main point of the sermon was being made. It's wrong to use culturally different images as it distorts your message, making you say something that you're not. In this case it was which party are you planning to vote for in the next US election – not do you want to follow God's way or your way? It's a very significant difference of tone just from one piece of clipart.

Another common mistake that people make is to use clipart from different sources. Once something is noticeable, it is a distraction, and if you have taken clipart drawn in different styles (such as a black and white woodcut mixed with a colourful cartoon figure with a big nose and comedy glasses) and used it in the same presentation, it instantly become a distraction. Use clipart sparingly and ask yourself if you really need to use it.

In the same service, the pastor also showed some video clips from a course that the church had been following. Again, it seemed that little thought had been put into how the extracts should be used. In both cases, the video was played until the preacher said, 'Right, you can stop it now'. How much more effective would it have been if he had marked out a stop point to the people on the video desk and asked them to fade it out at that point? It could have been even more embarrassing: if a film clip had been used, what would have happened if it had gone on beyond the intended extract and contained swear words, blasphemy or images that aren't intended for a family audience? Plan ahead – be careful in your choices and ensure that the people who know when to press play also know when to stop.

Preparing slides

So far we've focused on the visual ways in which you can use PowerPoint or similar programmes. Most people will use it for text summaries, and this also needs to be thought through carefully. Before typing a single word of your sermon notes on to PowerPoint or an OHP, you need to work out what is the most visible combination of typefaces, colours and words for the congregation you're going to speak to. If people can't read your words, then there's no point in wasting time producing them. Go into your church and look at where the screens are to be placed, find out where the blind spots are and where the sun comes in – will the glare blank out the screen? If so, then can the screen be moved to a place where it won't be affected by the sun?

When you've worked out the best position for the screen (or screens), then you'll need to work out the best way to present your text. If you're not offering handouts for people with visual impairments then you must ensure that every slide you offer is legible from the back. (If you don't offer handouts as a matter of course, shame on you. You should ensure that the stewards have some large-print handouts of each sheet to help people who wish to use them. This should form part of a church's response to the Disability Awareness Act of 2005, and will go a long way to making partially sighted visitors feel valued and welcome.)

The only way to find out what works is to test it. Prepare some slides that will allow you to see for yourself. As a rule of thumb, go for a minimum of 36 point text, choose a bold typeface and use a sans serif one, as this tends to be more legible from a distance. Never set your slides in capital letters: IT MAKES YOU LOOK LIKE YOU ARE SHOUTING AND IT'S HARDER TO READ. Use no more than six lines to a slide, especially if you are designing for a TV monitor. Remember, if you make it hard for people to read, you're going to make it harder for people to follow the service.

The colours you choose will also impact on members of the congregation. It is impossible for you to know if any of the people you will be speaking to are colour blind, so it's always a good idea to design slides as if they will be. The most common form of colour-blindness in the UK is an inability to tell the difference between red and green – so don't place green text on a red background. My church tends to use yellow letters on a burgundy or a bright blue background. Experiment and seek opinions, particularly from those in your fellowship who struggle to read.

Make sure that you design one format for the slides – one background, one typeface, one colour scheme – and be consistent. For example, if you've got a verse by verse Bible reading, don't make every verse fit one slide: a 15-verse reading should take as many slides as it needs with 36 point text on four lines, not 15 slides where the text is crammed in at different sizes. The same is true of song words – don't think you have to fit one verse to a slide – put the user first. Some software programmes, such as Presentation Manager, supply the song words; all you have to do is adapt the presentation to suit your church.

Take extra care on special occasions, such as welcoming new church members into the fellowship. These are the parts of services where people come to the front and set liturgy is taken from the denominational books, adding in the names at the appropriate points – 'We welcome _____ here today' – that type of thing. I've attended services where, for the benefit of the congregation, the liturgy has appeared on the big screen. Unfortunately, even though changing the text is easy, the people preparing the service didn't, so the text went up 'We welcome _____ here today, and he/she ...' More than anything else it suggests once again that the church doesn't care. Finally, if you have prepared a presentation, make sure that you have produced a printout for the people who press the buttons. Let them know what each slide is going to say, let them know what the cues are for changing them, for adding sound and video clips and turning things off. Don't assume that they will know – talk it through with them and let them raise any queries they might have about the sermon or presentation. Be prepared for things to go wrong and to be able to talk without the slides – you need to be able to deliver your sermon even if there's a power cut, the computer refuses to boot or the projector lights blow.

Above all, when planning your multimedia service, avoid anything that can form a distraction to the viewer. Watch out for spelling mistakes or missing words, check that the song words match up with what the worship group will be singing, and ensure that the verses are presented in the right order. We want people's attention focused on God, not human error.

SEVEN

BEING CREATIVE:
NOTICE SHEET DESIGN

Newsletters and notice sheets are probably the most overlooked ministry in the Church. We've looked at how the building, the signs, the people and services give a visitor their first impressions about a fellowship, but it is what they take away that will leave a lasting impression. A bad notice sheet and newsletter says 'We're a church that's making do', a dangerous attitude to take. In this chapter and the next, we'll look how to improve them – content and presentation – and look at how to reproduce them. We'll expand on the typography lesson from chapter 2 and the information about using images will act as a precursor to chapter 16.

Why notice sheets matter

In most churches, nestled inside the service books you'll find a sheet detailing that day's events, notification of forthcoming meetings and giving news of the fellowship. It's a useful piece of paper that helps the church function and draws people together. They're also used for sermon notes and act as bookmarks to Bible passages. So, it's important to get this right – a sheet that is full of unhelpful jargon, impenetrable code words and laid out without due care and attention will not endear itself to any newcomers. With a limited amount of space available and important information to convey, it has to hit the mark.

What is the sheet for?

Before anything else, the sheet needs to have a purpose. Is it to list the day's services and the forthcoming week? Is it specifically for that service and contains all readings, prayers and hymn details? Is it a combination of the two or is it for news of the fellowship? Your answer will also have to take into account whether the notice sheet complements, adds to or replaces a monthly magazine.

What information has to go in?

Start by deciding what the essential information is. It's usually details of that day's service, a note of welcome and a diary of the coming week. Then there's space for some more comprehensive notices, such as which guest speaker will be at the women's fellowship or which passages the home groups will study. Often, there is news from the fellowship, giving prayer pointers. Some churches also offer a short introduction to the day's theme via a minister's letter. Finally, there may be space for note taking.

Work out the format

Most notice sheets are a folded A4 sheet, giving four A5 pages. Another format used by some churches is an A4 sheet folded into thirds, producing a pamphlet. The downside to this format is the origami skills needed on opening – the reader must know which page order it goes in. If they are hand folded, they will take more time to produce. A local printer might be able to machine fold them for a modest fee, possibly discounted for a contract agreement for a set period of time. Some churches also choose to subscribe to an A4 news sheet called *Sunday Link*, produced by Redemptorist Publications (www.rpbooks.org). This weekly magazine sheet features a mixture of ecumenical comment, poems and cartoons touching on all aspects of the Church year. As it is inter-denominational, the material plays safe and will not cause offence. The reverse is left for churches to print their own service information. Other churches offer a single sheet of A5, produced on an A4 sheet of paper and then cut in half. There is no single right choice: each fellowship has to make a judgment based on their situation.

Work out how you want to say things

At first glance, this might seem like a strange heading: it's obvious – you want to say '10 a.m. Morning worship' and '6 p.m. Evening Worship'. Well, to a degree. Deciding on a house style will help plan the way the newsletter is to be designed.

The basic information could be:

'10.00 a.m. Morning Service with Joe Soap preaching. The Bible passage will be Genesis 1:1–17 and will be read by Mavis Bland. Flowers provided by Gertrude Arranger. Organist Geoff Tinkle. Children's activities run during service, organised by Ivor Trickortwo, looking at the parable of the Good Samaritan. After the service, refreshments in the church hall served by Jenny Sugar and Thomas Milk. 6 p.m. Evening Worship. Joe Soap preaches on John 20:17–22.'

This is a bit of a mouthful, and needs rationalising for speed reading; think of it as a *Radio Times* listing, something that gives a concise summary.

With some simple structuring, it can be changed:

Thank you for joining us as we worship God! These are details of today's services.

10 a.m. – Morning Worship led by the Revd Joe Soap

Genesis 1:1–17: A new beginning

Children will study the parable of the Good Samaritan. Please join us for refreshments after the service (servers: Jenny Sugar and Thomas Milk)

6 p.m. – Evening Worship led by the Revd Joe Soap

John 17:20-25: Praying for unity

Need prayer? Members of our prayer team will be at the front of the church after each service.

Today's flowers have been provided by Gertrude Arranger. They will be distributed after the service. If you know anyone who would welcome a bunch then please tell a steward on your way out.

This is much easier to digest than a huge chunk of information.

Likewise, if you have a diary of the week ahead, you can keep the information to the point – but you must make clear what each group is so that visitors can quickly work out if the group is relevant to them.

Monday

10 a.m. – Tumbletots (playgroup for ages 2–4). Large hall.

6.30 p.m. – Prayer meeting (to pray for missionaries). Pastor's office.

8 p.m. – Women's Guild (for all Christian women). Guest speaker Joe Soap reveals his top tips for a successful garden. Large hall.

Ensure that there are relevant contact details. Remember, this is a document that anyone can have access to, and you might prefer all enquiries to come through the church office. You should certainly never print the phone number and address of the church treasurer if they are taking the collection plate offering home after a service and sitting on it until they can go to the bank the following morning!

Most churches have now adopted the policy of only printing telephone numbers of their pastors and directing correspondence to the church office.

Make sure you also set the times as a.m. or p.m. While most people will be able to work out that an 8.00 prayer breakfast will be in the morning, it's a different matter for an 8.00 prayer meeting. Is that an early breakfast or a late tea? Don't leave things to chance. Also decide on a format for times – is it 8 a.m., 8.0 a.m. or 8.00 a.m.?

All this might seem rather insulting, but one church notice sheet I've collected actually listed its weekly diary as thus:

Monday	9.30–12.00	Coffee Stop
	12.15–1.0	Time of Prayer in Church
	7	Bible Study at Bloggschurch
Wednesday	1.00	Café Church
Thursday	11–2.00	Pop-In
	2.30	Guild – Speaker Mr. Joe Anglican

It's great that the church attempts to offer a range of activities during the week, but it's unclear what happens at each event, and who goes. The confusion is added to having three similar events: Monday's coffee stop, Wednesday's café church and Thursday's pop-in. If they are all offering the same thing to the same group of people, then the church would have been better to call it one and the same. If they are aimed at different audiences, such as the homeless, mothers or pensioners, then they could have been called 'new mums pop-in', 'pensioners' coffee stop' and so on.

Again, treat the notices like a *Radio Times* listing, an extra line explaining each event:

Monday

9.30 a.m.–noon – Coffee Stop   *A chance for new mums to enjoy a cuppa and get advice from a midwife.*

12.15 p.m.–1 p.m. – Time of prayer in church   *Focusing on missionaries supported by the church.*

7.30 p.m. – Bible study in the church   *A focus on Philemon, led by our pastor.*

Wednesday

1 p.m. – Café church   *Our café is open to the community to come and enjoy a hot lunch and some worship music.*

Thursday

11 a.m.–2 p.m. – Pop-in   *Refreshments, games, advice and a friendly ear for pensioners. All welcome.*

2.30 p.m. – Women's Guild   *Friendly meeting for all women, with special guest Joe Anglican talking about his butterfly collection.*

Want more details for any of these events? Call the church office on (01234) 567890.

It doesn't take much effort to be clear and concise, but it makes a world of difference.

Similarly, for announcements in the newsletter, you need to have a formula. You could consider group things under topics: youth matters, women's meetings, prayer meetings, matters for prayer and so on. Make sure that each notice is explanatory and also concise. Don't let people waffle. That's what I did the first time I called my church secretary to ask her to place a notice. After spending five minutes listening, she finally interrupted and asked what the announcement should say. Take time to work out the clearest and most concise way of saying something.

Here's an example:

'We're holding a church supper on Saturday, November 12 to raise funds for Helen's missionary work, offering a vegetarian and typical English fare plus a speaker from England Connect, Helen's missionary organisation. All welcome. It will be held in the large hall from 7 p.m. Numbers needed by November 5, you can give them to Nancy Cook. Call 123456 for details'

This is lengthy and clunky. Rearranging it slightly makes more sense:

Church supper to support missionary Helen Cole
Guest speaker from England Connect, Helen's organisation. Learn about her work in Barcelona over a traditional English meal (vegetarian options available). From 7 p.m. on Saturday, November 12. To book, call Nancy Cook on 123456 by November 5.

That's 60 words down to 44 without losing any sense and adding in some extra information about the location of Helen's missionary project.

Be very clear about what should go into the notice sheet, and what should go into the newsletter. Remember that both are public documents, read by different sections of the community. If personal details are given out, such as ex-directory phone numbers, permission must be sought. Any news about your missionaries must be written sensitively. Sermon notes should be written in gracious, rather than judgmental tones. Ensure that the notices are news, and not any old thing that just happens to be there – nor should there be reports that are several weeks old. Keep things fresh and up to date.

Beware the double entendre

Church newsletters are often the source of unintentional humour. Watch out for double meanings in concise notices, like these examples found on the Internet:

> 'This being Easter Sunday, we will ask Mrs Jones to come forward and lay an egg on the altar.'
>
> 'The 2003 Church Retreat will be hell May 10 and 11.'
>
> '"Weight Watchers" will meet at 7 p.m. in the church hall. Please use large double door at the side entrance.'

Work out the design

Having decided on both the format and the content, you can then decide on the style. This can be daunting at first, but it can also be fun, trying different typefaces out to get the most information in the clearest possible way.

Remember, it has to be readable for everyone and that will affect the way you choose to present the newsletter and the typefaces you choose. Your decision will need to be taken after testing a selection of different typefaces, both on the printer from which you will produce the final newsletter artwork and testing your church's reproduction machine, be it a photocopier or otherwise. This will be explained fully in the next chapter.

You'll also have to think of the needs of the fellowship: if you make it too small then people won't be able to read it. If you make it too large, then it will start to look amateurish. Your typeface should be from the corporate identity, as determined in chapter 2.

To brighten up the newsletter, you can add some small illustrations: there is a selection of different clip art collections available both via the Internet and from Christian bookshops. Use a range that is in the same style. Mixing different art styles is noticeable and reflects badly on the fellowship.

Collinstone Community Church decided to use Officina: it comes in two complementary typefaces, Officina Serif and Officina Sans. On this page you'll see a front page and a page of notices from its notice sheet taking all this into account.

Ensure that there are a few large print version of the notice sheet with the stewards. These will be invaluable for those who need them. To create these sheets, you'll usually need to use a photocopier, enlarging up in proportion – either A5 to A4, or A4 to A3.

Collinstone Community Church

Sunday, November 5

Thank you for joining us today as we worship God. We hope you are made to feel welcome.

Today's services

9am Morning worship
with Tara McNee looking at Romans 1.

10.30am Morning worship led by Andrew Stammers looking at Encouragement. Reading: 1 Kings 15.
Groups for children and teenagers will meet during the service. A creche is available and a baby changing room is available at the back of the church. For details, ask a steward.
After the service, coffee will be served by the Johnstone Road housegroup.

6.30pm Evening worship led by Watson Holmes.
Focus on prayer and spiritual gifts.

8pm Teenage after-church in the small hall.

Need prayer? After each service, a member of our prayer team will be availble to pray with you. They will be in the prayer corner at the front of the church.

Is this your first time here?
We warmly welcome you and thank you for coming.
Please join us for refreshments after the service. We have a range of small groups available should you wish to join one for.

Are you a 'carer'
Are you a 'carer' – someone whose lifestyle is significantly affected by caring for someone else? If you need prayer or help, please contact Joan Smith (contact details from church office) and we will do what we can. If you need cleaning help (for example), please check the offers on the notice board; or feel free to advertise there yourself. (Obviously the church can't guarantee the services advertised there.)
Can you help someone else in Collinstone? If you can help sometimes with cleaning (either paid or unpaid), shopping, cooking, gardening, DIY, or driving, please contact Joan.

Cake makers
Couple's Course needs cakes on Thursday evenings for the next 12 weeks.
Can you help? Ring Vicki Foreman.

Job vacancy
Community Action is looking for a part-time paid advice worker, offering help and assistance to people with money or health problems. See the job vacancies notice board for more details.

Are planning to run the half-marathon?
Are you taking part in either the Collinstone Half Marathon or the London Marathon? If so, why not consider running it for Community Action? We will provide sponsorship forms and a very fetching T-shirt for you to wear!
Contact Ian or Barbara via the Community Action office, or by calling 123456.

Actors wanted for new play
The CCC drama group is planning a new play that adapts the story of the good Samaritan as a Western. If you are interested in taking part, come to the auditions after the 10.45am service on Sunday. If you would like to be there but can't make it or have any other queries, contact Magnus Jacobs on 123456 or by emailing: m.jacobs@mailserve.com.uk.

Can you feed some students?
Help needed to provide baguette lunches for the University's Christian Union lunch time evangelistic talks. These take place on Tuesdays at 1pm and are a great way for students to learn more about following Jesus. If you can help or need further information, contact Ruth Silvester by calling 123456 or by emailing: r.silvester06@collinstone.ac.uk.

Prayer diary
The church's monthly prayer diary is now available on the welcome desk, along with other prayer resources from Christian organisations.

The final stages

When printing the final artwork, it would be prudent – for reasons of clarity – to use a laser printer and not an inkjet printer. This will give crisper text that will be easier for the eye to read. Similarly, you will get a better result by using a slightly heavier weight of paper. Normal office photocopier paper is 80gsm (and perfect for reproducing the final sheets), but switching to a 100gsm paper for the artwork will enhance the quality of the print, especially if you duplicate the notice sheet on a Risograph machine – these are perfect for medium size print runs but its drawback is that the ink starts to 'fill in' – so the text appears blacker than it looks. This is why it's important to run tests of your machine before changing the design – you have to know what it's going to look like.

If your notice sheet is an A5 page that has been printed two-up (two pages side-by-side) on an A4 sheet of paper, make sure that you trim the paper properly. It's surprisingly common to pick up notice sheets that have been messily folded in half or poorly cut. Sometimes the paper hasn't been placed into the guillotine properly, and the result is a notice sheet that has a jagged cut line – it can be diagonal, rather than straight. Again, it's a minor thing but it makes the church look unprofessional and as if it doesn't care about what goes out in its name. The best way to cut your A4 notice sheet into A5 is to take it to a local printer and ask them to trim the pages. It will take them a couple of minutes and cost you no more than a couple of quid.

Making these simple changes will help give your church a useful notice sheet that its readers will value and appreciate.

EIGHT

HOLD THE FRONT PAGE: MAKING YOUR NEWSLETTER A MUST-READ

Newsletters are one of the most important pieces of church communication. Most of the information about a church comes from the magazine. So why are most of them snoozeletters? Over the years, I've seen hundreds of them. Labours of love, these efforts are crafted in people's spare time and you can sense the blood, sweat and tears that went into them. But reading a newsletter from a church you've never been to is like gate-crashing a dinner party; they're full of in-jokes, acronyms and articles that make no sense to anyone but the author. And they can convey a sense of desperation that small, under-resourced churches often have. Turning them around can be quite simple – all it takes is some forward planning.

Real-life examples

Here are some excerpts from newsletters around the country (all names have been changed).

Bring a Friend Day

Members of SPRING are being encouraged to bring a friend to join us on this day between 10 and 11.30 a.m. Could you give a warm invitation to someone you know? Any carer with pre-school children will be welcome.
Want to know more? See Zoe, Victoria or Liz.

What is Spring? Why should they invite friends? Why is it a special occasion? And who are Zoe, Victoria or Liz?

The Written Word

Reading is one of my passions, and the variety of subject matter seems endless. The thing about reading is that whatever book, I instinctively get inside it; I enter into it in a very personal way and I am transported to my interpretation of what the author is saying. One such book I read was *Treasure Island* by Robert Louis Stevenson. His grasp of family matters is unique and very perceptive.

After three paragraphs, the article starts. And it's not about a book – it's an opportunity for the author to write that they believe in God.

One newsletter devoted eight pages of text to the diary of a member who had spent a gap year teaching English abroad. Naturally, they wrote about their week's holiday, not their year's work. 'Highlights' included spending an hour looking for a phone box, finding a hotel and ordering drinks with a meal. It came after eight pages of very dry AGM reports. Another newsletter featured an appreciation in lieu of an obituary, written by the husband of the deceased. Sadly, not once did the article mention who she was, what she'd done or how she died. Instead, it was a very personal monologue of her husband's fondest memories.

Finally, one church newsletter opened with a four-page article detailing the progress of a committee set up to move the church on with new projects and visions. Featuring numerous spelling mistakes and meaningless jargon, it is impossible to say what the vision is. You'd learn more from the corner shop next door.

In all these cases, a little thought and some gentle editing could have transformed these newsletters.

Who is it for?

All magazines are tailored to a specific audience: you don't get many pony fans buying *Tropical Fish Weekly.* Magazine editors know what their audience wants – working from market research and readers' feedback. Knowing their subject area, they'll also work with their instinct. This applies to your church newsletter; it needs a clearly defined aim. On a basic level, it's either aimed at regular attendees of the church or it's a form of outreach that brings the church closer to the community. There is no middle ground as the decision you make affects the way in which the newsletter should be produced.

Given the choice, always go for the external communications option, because you never know who will read it. While you know where the newsletter starts off, what happens to it when it leaves the church is an unknown. It's highly likely that your church's neighbours, even those who don't go, will regard the church as their local, simply because it's on their doorstep. This will be especially true for Church of England and Catholic fellowships, because the majority of people in Britain regard themselves as one or the other. People are naturally curious

about their local church, whether they go or not. Picking up
the newsletter is the easiest way of finding out without asking.
Is your church's newsletter collected from a table at the back
of the church hall? Is a copy carefully given to everyone in
the fellowship? Do volunteers go out round the community
and deliver it from door to door? Is the newsletter left in local
Post Offices or village stores for people to collect? Could any
of this be changed?

To charge or not to charge?

Church newsletters aren't cheap. If a church is producing 100
16-page A5 size magazines a month, that's almost a ream
of paper, plus duplicating costs. It has to be paid for, so it's
natural that churches would want to claw this back. Treat the
newsletter as part of the church's outreach and evangelism
ministry and bring it under that budget. Hold fundraising
events to pay for it. Reduce the frequency to bi-monthly. Keep
the page count to the minimum. Use a thinner weight of paper.
Solicit advertisements or sponsorship from local businesses.
But don't ask people to pay for it: it's a ministry.

The great sins of newsletters

Before putting a new style newsletter together, we need to
understand what newsletters are routinely doing wrong. Here
are some of the most common errors plucked from a random
selection of the nation's newsletters.

Terrible editorial

Often, you can sense the editor's desperation as the deadline
for the magazine flies past and the only submitted articles are

the minister's letter and the diary dates. So any old rubbish gets shoved in as it was written by people in the fellowship. It's like having to sit through a stranger's holiday snaps, only less interesting.

One cover design, different coloured paper

We are surrounded by images. Modern technology means it's easy to incorporate them into any computer-generated print out. So why do churches insist on using the same cover every edition?

Sloppy production standards

A common mistake is to avoid proofreading pages – words are left out, spelling blunders are left in and names and dates are wrong. However, all kinds of errors creep in because no one checked: there are pages where a headline is at the bottom of one page and the accompanying article is on the next. Alternatively, the final half-word of a paragraph is poking out of the top of the following page. Some also reprint whole pages in the same issue.

Impenetrable in-jokes, acronyms and names

Not everyone knows who Jill or Clare is, or why they're behind PUSH. Just because you do, not everyone else will. Use internal jargon and you'll put people off the magazine and the church.

Articles don't know when to start or stop

We rely a lot on visual signposting when going through a publication: headlines, pictures, section headings all help us work out were we are. So if a magazine reads like one long letter, it's harder to dip in and out of. Help your readers by keeping articles at set lengths. No article in a church newsletter should be any longer than four A5 pages – that's about 1,600 words.

Terrible pictures

Church magazines still tend to use clip art of all different shapes and sizes that are vaguely suitable. Likewise, some newsletters try and use photographs where it's impossible to know who's who as they are dark, blurred, unclear or unlabelled.

Starting again

Editors periodically review the content of their publication, deciding whether tweaks are needed (such as a change of columnist or a new headline typeface) or a root and branch change is necessary. Little changes help a paper evolve. The problem is that readers have a sense of ownership towards their periodical: there was a massive outcry when the *Radio Times* moved its radio listings from the television, creating a separate section. Now, if the editor were to move them back there would be a similar outcry. Therefore changes need to be planned, not done on a whim.

Remembering the importance of your church newsletter as an outreach tool, you will need to take a critical eye to it. Make a list of the range of articles it's carried over the past year. For example, the church leader might have written a letter. That could have taken up two or three sides of A5. You might have had a diary page each month, three pages of reports from missionaries. Someone might have written a feature about their hobby that used four pages. And so on. Looking back will help you look forward. Research other magazines: women's weeklies, men's magazines, lifestyle magazines. Look at the range of issues they cover, how they cover them, what they think is important. See how much space they devote to different issues, and how they explain difficult concepts, such as a medical condition. Make a note of the things that you like or dislike. Talk about these magazines with people from your church: you can determine a new direction for the magazine by airing likes and dislikes.

The Baptist Men's Movement wrote a paper about a redesign of its publication, *World Outlook*, after researching lads' magazines. One of the conclusions was that its magazine 'addresses some of the issues that young men would identify with. However its [current] style and presentation could be off-putting.' So the problem facing the magazine was one of style as well as substance.

You also need to know your readership. This is the hardest part of all, as readership of a church magazine should be the entire church with a cross-section of ages, sexes, earning potential, social class and reading ability. But you will be able to determine some specifics. Your church's situation will take on an importance here – there is little point in writing a review about a Christian rap CD if the majority of your church is elderly or having a children's page if you have no children in the church. If the magazine is delivered to your local estate, then look at how that is made up: is it an area with a wide ethnic diversity? Is it an area of excessive unemployment? Are there a lot of young mums close by?

Analysing your magazine's content, the content of secular magazines and the needs of your readership will help give you a sense of direction. Discussing it with a panel from your church will help plan the kind of magazine you want to be. Will you include testimonies, tips for mothers, recipes, ideas for computers – all written from a Christian perspective? Or will it be a digest of the events that have happened in your fellowship since the last issue was published? What suits one church will not suit another – that's why this research matters. It might seem a very thorough exercise for a simple church magazine but it's worth it because it will give your newsletter a greater sense of purpose than just printing every submitted article. You devalue both your efforts and your newsletter if you think it's just a newsletter for your local church and it doesn't matter very much.

Planning the content

'Copy for the next edition should reach me NOT LATER than November 23, earlier if possible.' To avoid this begging note, plan ahead. Instead of waiting for copy to come to you, be pro-active and commission articles; give the authors a brief to follow and a word count. In doing so, you will make the production of an issue much easier.

KNOW HOW MANY WORDS FIT A PAGE

Having chosen a design, work out the number of words to a page in the typefaces you have chosen. For example, an A5 page in one typeface will contain about four hundred words of text. If you had a feature article with a picture, then you could spread this over two pages and have about five to six hundred words. Small news items could be anything from fifty to one hundred and fifty words each. This small piece of knowledge will help you as you decide the content of the issue.

PLAN THE ISSUE

I always start with my back of an envelope issue plan, before making it final. I'll sketch down the numbers 1 to 16 on separate lines. Between the odd and even numbers I'll add a rule so I know which pages are facing pages: 1 is a page by itself, but page 2 faces page 3, 4 faces page 5 etc. The centre spread is similarly flagged up as the article can go all the way across the centre (the fold). This is the book, the pages before the fold are at the front of the book, the pages after are the back of the book.

Now take a tip from how red-top newspapers are structured: page three is just as important as the front page. It's known as the second front page, and contains interesting and eye-grabbing news or pictures. In most tabloids, there is solid news all the way through to the fold. It's then a mixture of features, classifieds, television and sport. Adapt this for your church newsletter, consider opening with a strong feature on page three (a testimony or interview with someone in your fellowship perhaps) rather than the traditional minister's letter. Where should the letter go? For most churches, this is the important editorial comment. Its position might be on page two, it might be at the back. Should it be used as a great slab of text on your second front page? No. So, to go back to our fictitious example, we will have a three page feature starting on page 3, with a strong headline, a picture and minimal text that encourage us to turn over to read the rest of the article. *Reader's Digest* uses this method – look at their magazine for inspiration.

Page 6 will be the minister's letter. Pages 7–10 will become a pull-out section: the church's diary. Page 7 will list that month's Sunday services: the preacher and readings. Pages 8 and 9 can be a calendar style month, showing what's happening on each day, such as the example overleaf:

					March 2006	
Sunday	**Monday**	**Tuesday**	**Wednesday**	**Thursday**	**Friday**	**Saturday**
			1 8 p.m. House Groups	**2** 11 a.m. Bible Study 12 noon Church Lunch 2.30 p.m. Woman's Meeting 7.30 p.m. Table Tennis 8.30 p.m. Worship Group	**3** 7 - 8 a.m. Mens Prayer Breakfast in lecture room 8 p.m. Singing Group	**4** 7.30 a.m. CTW Prayer & Praise in the lecture room
5 9.45 a.m. Prayer Meeting 10.30 a.m. Family Worship 6.30 p.m. Evening Worship with Communion	**6** 2 - 3 p.m. Sunbeams for under 5's 5.30 - 9.15 p.m. Girl's Brigade 5.45 - 9 p.m. Boy's Brigade at Woosehill	**7** 10 a.m. 4321 2 p.m. Prayer Group 8 p.m. House Group	**8** 8 p.m. House Groups	**9** Easter Experience 11 a.m. Bible Study at 1 7.30 p.m. Table Tennis 8.30 p.m. Worship Group	**10** 7 - 8 a.m. Mens Prayer Breakfast in lecture room Easter Experience 8 p.m. Singing Group	**11** 7 p.m. Fairtrade Feast at St Pauls Parish Rooms
12 9.45 a.m. Prayer Meeting 10.30 a.m. Morning Worship **12 Noon Magazine Deadline** 4 p.m. Afternoon Service 6.30 p.m. Evening Worship	**13** 2 - 3 p.m. Sunbeams for under 5's 5.30 - 9.15 p.m. Girl's Brigade 5.45 - 9 p.m. Boy's Brigade at Woosehill	**14** 10 a.m. 4321 2 p.m. Prayer Group 8 p.m. House Group	**15** 7.45 p.m. CTW Lent Course at All Saints 8 p.m. House Groups	**16** 11 a.m. Bible Study 2.30 p.m. Women's Meeting 7.30 p.m. Table Tennis 8.30 p.m. Worship Group	**17** 7 - 8 a.m. Mens Prayer Breakfast in lecture room 8.30 a.m. Intercessory Prayer Meeting in Lecture Room 8 p.m. Singing Group	**18**
19 9.45 a.m. Prayer Meeting 10.30 a.m. Morning Worship 6.30 p.m. Evening Worship	**20** 2 - 3 p.m. Sunbeams for under 5's 5.30 - 9.15 p.m. Girl's Brigade 5.45 - 9 p.m. Boy's Brigade at Woosehill	**21** 10 a.m. 4321 2 p.m. Prayer Group 8 p.m. Church Meeting	**22** 7.45 p.m. CTW Lent Course at All Saints 8 p.m. House Groups	**23** 11 a.m. Bible Study 2.30 p.m. Woman's Meeting 7.30 p.m. Table Tennis 8.30 p.m. Worship Group	**24** 7 - 8 a.m. Mens Prayer Breakfast in lecture room 8 p.m. Singing Group	**25**
26 9.45 a.m. Prayer Meeting 10.30 a.m. Morning Worship 6.30 p.m. Evening Worship	**27** 2 - 3 p.m. Sunbeams for under 5's 5.30 - 9.15 p.m. Girl's Brigade 5.45 - 9 p.m. Boy's Brigade at Woosehill	**28** 10 a.m. 4321 2 p.m. Prayer Group 8 p.m. House Group	**29** 7.45 p.m. CTW Lent Course at All Saints 8 p.m. House Groups	**30** 11 a.m. Bible Study 2.30 p.m. Women's Meeting 7.30 p.m. Table Tennis 8.30 p.m. Worship Group	**31** 7 - 8 a.m. Mens Prayer Breakfast in lecture room 8 p.m. Singing Group	

Page 10 can become the rotas and contact details. In this format, people can pull it out and keep. Pages 11–13 can be three pages of news from the fellowship, such as young people's groups, news of the church meetings, visits made to official church events. Page 14 can be another feature – news from the church's missionaries perhaps – 15 a crossword and 16 a children's page.

That list can then be turned into a flat plan – a sheet of paper where each page is represented by a matchbox sized rectangle. Pages are drawn together as pairs, again to help visualise which ones face each other.

Commissioning articles

The editor needs to find out what's coming up in the church. Some things will be easier than others: you might know that the church is raising funds for a missionary, but knowing that the youth group will be awarding prizes needs the organiser to get in touch with you. Or, the editor can call leaders of church groups periodically looking for news. In a large church this responsibility should be shared or the church council should offer advice as it will know what's coming up. If you encourage the leaders to get in contact with you in advance, then they will eventually get into the habit of letting you know.

Once an article is commissioned, allocate space for it. Always ask for more words than you need and warn the contributor that it might be edited down. Each article needs to answer the questions *Who? What? When? Where?* and *Why?* and not be a rambling diary entry. Does this mean that there's no space for old news (say a Christmas report in the June edition)? Make space for interesting articles, that's the best rule. Obviously the longer an article is left the more out of date it is.

Give writers a brief

If you're asking for a report on a teenager receiving a major Boys' Brigade honour, then think about what your readers will want to know. Who is the boy, what is the award, why has he received it, what has he done to earn it, when and where will he obtain it, who was present at the awards? Will there also be pictures taken of him receiving the honour? A small report like this should be worth between one hundred and fifty and two hundred words and focus on what he did to obtain the award. This should be sufficient information for your Boys' Brigade leader to go away and write the report. Be explicit about what you are expecting – you might feel like a dictator, but if you want to have a consistent magazine it's a necessary evil.

Find out how they can deliver their copy to you

Most people can now email their report, saved as a word processing document. Encourage them to cut and paste the article to the body of the email and to save the text in a format that you can read. There is no point in receiving a Publisher file when you can only open a Word file. If they don't have a computer, ask for typewritten copy on clean paper, it should be possible to save retyping time by scanning the text and using character recognition software: proofread it before printing! If they have to submit handwritten copy, ask for neat writing and all names to be spelt in capitals. How they submit their copy will have a bearing on their deadline: there is less work if they email it to you.

Give a deadline earlier than you need it – but don't let on!

Ask for something earlier than it's needed as it builds in an extra period of grace should you be let down. You have time to find something else or do some gentle nagging. Don't be afraid to call your correspondent and find out where the copy is: there might be a genuine reason, but people usually need prompting. There is nothing to be embarrassed about if they agreed to your deadline. And never let on about this period of grace.

Work with the author over any changes

People sometimes ignore your brief and write what they feel like. This can be acceptable, but the article may need reworking. If you have enough time before the issue goes to the printers, ask them to make the changes. You will need some diplomatic skills here: be encouraging, not a bully. No one gets paid for producing a church newsletter, so don't take people for granted. Also be firm and fair and hold on to the editor's right to amend copy as needed.

Design the newsletter clearly

The majority of newsletters I've seen tend to stick to one layout: a random selection of typefaces with headings underlined at the same point size as the rest of the text and with every first letter capitalised. It's dull and boring.

Here's an example:

<u>Church Visit To Ancient Abbey</u>

Lorem ipsum dolor sit amet, consectetuer adipiscing elit. Nullam ligula. Duis ligula nisl, egestas in, tristique tempus, nonummy a, orci. Pellentesque bibendum purus sagittis est.

How much more interesting a page looks if a heading is easy to spot:

Abbey visit brings history alive

Lorem ipsum dolor sit amet, consectetuer adipiscing elit. Nullam ligula. Duis ligula nisl, egestas in, tristique tempus, nonummy a, orci. Pellentesque bibendum purus sagittis est.

Using a large size of typeface will break up the page and create a lively easy-to-read layout. The headline has also changed: it's interesting and not just factual, making you ask, 'What history has been brought alive?'

Get the layout right

The layout of the newsletter plays a key role in whether people want to read it or not. Although design can be subjective, having consistent typography is important. A newsletter requires long-distance reading: Each article is for reading rather than just scanning quickly. It therefore suits a serif typeface, which has been designed to be read at length. The only way to find a typeface that suits your publication is to try some out. Gauge reaction from people in the church – different sizes, increase the line spacing (less words per page, but can be more legible).

Remember the importance of line length and leading: consider using several columns across the page – two for an A5 page, three for an A4 one. Get the amount of white space right and help your readers. There's more advice on this in chapter 2.

Cover stars

What do you want to appear on the cover? A magazine needs a good masthead – that's the magazine title. It should also have as little essential information as possible. 'The magazine of Collinstone Community Church' 'November 2007' are probably the only things that need to appear here. Many churches choose to have incredibly dull covers, using pictures of their church (or bizarrely, a clip art picture of a building that could be a factory, it's hard to tell) and nothing else. The best church magazine cover I've seen is Stanmore Baptist Church's *LinkLines*. A member of the church is an artist and she provides an illustration of the local area each month. Her sketches are ideal to be reproduced in black and white, and combined with a Bible verse they make exciting covers. What could your church do? Now that reproducing artwork is easier, thanks to modern technology, there is no excuse for churches to stick to one cover design and just change the date and the coloured paper used for the cover. Photographically gifted members could take pictures; use inspirational pictures from clip art collections; choose a Bible verse and illustrate it typographically; create a women's magazine-style cover using a member of the congregation; encourage gifted artists; use a picture of an event that took place in the church recently ... the possibilities are endless.

Using photos

Reproducing pictures in a church magazine is one of the hardest parts of the job. Old technology prevented us from using pictures as they wouldn't come out clearly – everything had to be a line drawing. All this is changing and new duplication machines are capable of reproducing a picture. But before using pictures, you'll need to calibrate your printer to give you the best original artwork. Buying an inkjet printer is a waste of money. The initial price for a good inkjet printer might make it seem cheaper, but the ink costs more than champagne and you'll get more pages from a toner cartridge in a laser printer, saving money in the long term.

Buy the best laser printer you can afford – A4-sized colour machines are now retailing around the £200 mark, but the colour toner cartridges are about £80 each and they use four (cyan, magenta, yellow and black). Even a good quality mono printer will cost you about £150, with £70 per cartridge. Talk to a computer expert for advice on the right printer for your church office.

Cost aside, laser printers give sharper originals. Inkjet printouts can smudge, and the amount of black ink on a page

can pucker the paper. To get the best out of your printer, you
need to produce a printer test sheet – my version is available
to download on the ditchthedayglo.co.uk website, and is
reproduced here.

At the top of the page, it features 10 squares, featuring a shade
of grey (10 per cent black, 20 per cent black and so on) with

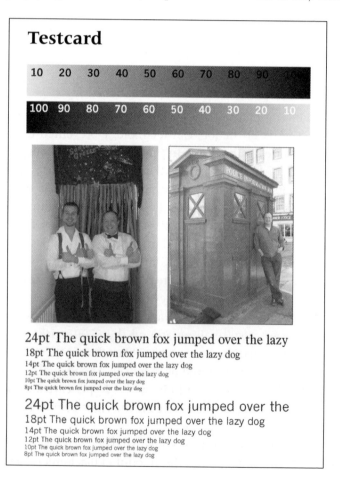

the percentage written in black in the middle of the box. This is then repeated going down, but with white writing. This tests the tonal range of the printer and your duplicator, as there will be a point at which text and box are indistinguishable.

Underneath that are two colour contrasted pictures – one with a border and one without. Some sample lines of text are repeated at different point sizes to see at what point they start to break up and become illegible. Recreate this sheet, print it from the printer that produces the magazine's master pages and then duplicate it a dozen times. Keep these charts as reference points.

Make sure it's straight

When printing your final artwork, ensure that the paper is straight. The eye will notice if the text is at a different angle to the bottom of the page, making it harder to read.

Reproduction equipment

Use the best quality machine you can. Don't let it run out of toner or ink and think 'that'll do.' There are some specialist magazine printers, such as parishmagprinters.co.uk who print church newsletters for a reasonable price. If the magazine is printed by an outside company, then it means you won't need volunteers to collate, fold and staple the magazine, saving on valuable time in the church office.

Alternative ideas

Your church newsletter doesn't have to be an A5-sized black and white magazine with a small print run. Some churches will print their magazine as A4 pages, and this change in size offers more versatility in layout terms but will cost more to produce. The ultimate in outreach tools, however, is to produce your own newspaper. Many local newspapers offer contract printing services and are willing to produce a small newspaper for you to deliver to your neighbourhood. Limitations will vary from printing press to printing press, but expect to produce eight tabloid pages and produce a minimum of around 5,000 with a run-on price per extra 1,000. Availability of colour will depend on the press, but it is becoming increasingly common for newspapers to be able to print back-to-back colour (colour on every page). This approach is perfect to deliver to every home in your neighbourhood, but it will have to be a professional product. The newspaper company might be able to help, or print from files that you have created.

Load the magazine onto your church's website

Let the magazine be part of your church's website: it can give would-be visitors a flavour of the fellowship. It's also a way of keeping in touch with your missionaries and saving paper. Remember that the Internet is a public space and anyone can access your church's website – so don't upload sensitive information. For more on this, see Chapter 12.

Resources

You're not on your own. There are a variety of different sources available on the Internet to help you. Logging on to www.ditchthedayglo.co.uk will enable you to access the newsletter forums, where you can ask questions, discuss articles with others and also seek advice. A variety of websites offer copy for your magazine – www.parishpump.co.uk offers a wide range of material for an annual subscription, but the content is centred on the Church of England. Another resource is www.thesheepdip.co.uk, which offers a range of articles including news, puzzles and celebrity articles, but on a pay-as-you-go basis or subscription fee. Parishmagprinters.co.uk offers help and advice, especially with reproducing your magazine. I have used them and always found them willing to help. There is also a 'trade body' for newsletter editors: the Association of Church Newsletter Editors. Its website, www.ac-editors.co.uk, offers a forum and they have regular meetings.

A newsletter should reflect well on the church it represents, be entertaining and inspiring to its readers and be relevant to the situation that the fellowship is in. If it is encouraging, then it will be an invaluable outreach tool for your neighbourhood.

NINE

PAPER TIPS: CHURCH STATIONERY

Designing a letterhead

Everyone likes to receive a letter, especially as now, thanks to email, it's more of a novelty. Letters are lasting, emails are often quickly deleted. Church stationery creates a first impression much like the welcomers on a church door do; the welcomer is conveyed through the paper, ink, typefaces and layout. So why do churches often neglect the importance of these publicity tools?

Through my work, I've seen a large selection of church letterheads: most are now individually produced from inkjet printers. A few are at least 20 years old and have details of former pastors and phone numbers crossed out by hand. A tiny minority of them are professionally produced, making them stand out for the wrong reason.

To understand what makes a good letterhead, it's vital to know what a bad one is like. Here are two fictitious examples based on real letterheads. The first, from Collinstone Chapel URC/Baptist Partnership, uses seven different typefaces, when just one or two are needed. At the top of the letterhead are the names of the two ministers, one on the left, the other on the right – in noticeably different fonts. One minister's name is listed as 'Rev. Roger Andrews', the other's 'Rev Peter Anderson'. One phone number is '(01234) 567890', the other is '(01234) 098765'. The church's slogan has a spacing mistake in it – 'God so love s the'. Finally, there is no address for the church itself.

Collinstone Chapel Collinstone

Rev. Roger Andrews
123 Any Street
Collinstone
Rutland
CZ1 2BC
Tel: (01234)567890
rogerandrews@email.co.com

United Reformed / Baptist Chapel

For God so love s the world that he gave his only Son, that whoever
believes in him should not perish but have eternal life

Rev Peter Anderson
321 Madeup Road
Collinstone
Rutland
CZ1 2BC
Tel: (01234) 098765
revpete@searchme.com

The second letterhead, from Collinstone Baptist Church, uses five different typefaces. The actual letterhead was a seventh generation photocopy of an original letterhead: you can tell from the way the line drawing of the church had deteriorated over time.

COLLINSTONE BAPTIST CHURCH

Green Street, Collinstone, CZ1 2BC

Church Office: (01234) 567890
E-mail: Andrew McBrown
colliboffice@email.co.com

Even though this letterhead has been photocopied, at the bottom of the page the names of two former church officers have been crossed out. If the photocopy was recent, those details should have been blanked out. And instead of stockpiling photocopies, it should have been printed: a printing company would have created artwork that matched and looks professional.

Here's what it could have looked like had it been tidied up:

COLLINSTONE BAPTIST CHURCH

Green Street, Collinstone, CZ1 2BC
Church Office: (01234) 567890
E-mail: collibcoffice@email.co.com

The design of the church stationery isn't the only issue. The choice of paper it is printed on also matters – a photocopied letterhead is less professional than a letterhead that has been printed on better paper. Standard office paper is usually white 80gsm (photocopy paper), but there are hundreds of different types. The most famous brand is Conqueror and your local print shop will be able to suggest (cheaper) alternatives. Although most letterheads are now printed on white paper, usually at 100gsm, the entire rainbow is available; your printer will have samples. Although it will cost a little extra, it will be worth it. It doesn't even have to be a brand name: simply switching to 100gsm will make a difference as people notice the change in paperweight.

If you feel that you can't afford to have letterheads printed, and they must be photocopied or produced each time from your printer, then you can easily buy 100gsm paper from an office supply shop. Shop around for the best prices and deals.

Why print a letterhead professionally, when it's cheaper to photocopy?

Photocopying might seem like a good deal, especially if you have a small church. And with a good photocopier, it's acceptable. But there is a noticeable difference between the printing process, which uses ink, and a photocopier, which uses toner. A photocopier also requires the paper to be kept dry – if it gets damp (usually when it's stored outside of a waxed-lined paper wrapper) then it can jam in the copier. This seems a little far-fetched, but it can happen. One big advantage of having the letterheads printed professionally is that you can use colour, be it full colour or a single one – there are thousands to choose from. Most printers work with a colour matching system called Pantone®. It's worth discussing your colour choices with your printers; they can show you samples and give their advice.

The more letterheads you have printed, the cheaper they become: if 100 cost £25 and 500 costs £50, it's obviously more economical to go for the larger quantity. The reason is that the first 100 includes set-up costs – the printing plates, preparing the ink and ensuring the colour registration is correct. Once that's done, it's easy for the printer to continue the run.

Why not use an inkjet printer?

If you have set up your word processing programme with a suitable letter heading, then you might want to simply print out a new letterhead every time you need one. This can be perfectly acceptable, but the danger is that with the wrong choice paper, your design becomes noticeable. Too thin (that includes 80gsm) and the ink creases the paper and can be seen from the reverse. If the paper is laid ('The series of horizontal and vertical lines is a reminder of a time when paper was handmade' the Conqueror website explains) then the ink doesn't sit well on the paper, appearing to be blotchy. It's a matter of perception: if letterheads are professionally printed, they reflect well on the church.

Why not use a laser printer?

The downside to printing a letter heading from a laser printer is that it will be black and white, unless you pay extra for a colour printer. Like a photocopier, a laser printer works by using toner to imprint the image to the page, so this method relies on you ensuring there is enough toner in the printer. Again, there is a noticeable difference to the letterhead because it's not printed with ink, but it's acceptable if you're on a budget.

A letterhead needs your contact details

It must include the name of the church, the address and contact details for the church (phone and fax number, email and website). Whether you include details of church leaders, treasurers and administrators is up to you. The best compromise option is to have the contact details for the church office, but have a 'reply to:' part printed on the top right of the letterhead. Produce a suitable template for your word processing software, share it with those who will produce church-related correspondence. They can use this template to add in their details when writing their letter. While this isn't the prettiest route to go down, it will enable you to order a cost-effective number of letterheads without wasting any if someone moves away.

TONE BAPTIST CHURCH

Green Street, Collinstone, CZ1 2BC
Church Office: (01234) 567890
E-mail: collibcoffice@email.co.com

Reply to: The Revd Roger Andrews,
123 Any Street,
Collinstone,
CZ1 2BC

Legal requirements

The legal requirements of a letterhead depend on the nature of your church: talk to your printer at the time of placing an order, or visit the Government's website, www.businesslink.gov.uk, although the advice is mainly for businesses. Small traders need a VAT registration number on invoices, partnerships need the names of all partners and limited companies must show the name of the company, the country of registration, the company registration number, the address of the registered office and the address of its place of business, if different. Under section 68 of the Charities Act 1993, a charitable company whose name does not include the word charity or charitable must state the fact that it is a charity (including its charity registration number) on all materials it sends out.

How should they be designed?

There is no set way – it's very much a matter of taste. The basic option is simply a block of text, all in the same size typeface centred at the top of the page. This is very dull and looks old-fashioned and like private correspondence, not a 'business' letter.

Your church should have a logo and a corporate identity (see chapter 2), which will give you a starting point for any letterhead. The name of the church must dominate, be it through the logo or the colours used. It should also be in a larger typesize than anything else on the page.

The first example letterhead in this chapter, for Collinstone Chapel, Collinstone is a cluttered layout and very boring. Listing the two ministers without saying who is who (is one a Baptist or one a senior pastor?) is a no-no. If you want to include this information on your letterhead, then think about the layout of the sheet. The name of the church could be centred, with the motto underneath it. Underneath that, the address of the church and the names and addresses of the ministers can either be left off or moved to the bottom of the page. It depends on whether more business is done in the manse or the church office.

Collinstone Chapel Collinstone

Rev. Roger Andrews
123 Any Street
Collinstone
Rutland
CZ1 2BC
Tel: (01234)567890
rogerandrews@email.co.com

United Reformed / Baptist Chapel

For God so love s the world that he gave his only Son, that whoever
believes in him should not perish but have eternal life

Rev Peter Anderson
321 Madeup Road
Collinstone
Rutland
CZ1 2BC
Tel: (01234) 098765
revpete@searchme.com

This is the original. Simply by restructuring the way the information is presented, we can create an elegant letter-head (opposite).

This is easier for the eye, and has clear signposting: the name of the church first, then the verse and contact details at the bottom. However, it looks very bland. By changing the layout further and inserting a picture of the church, we can project a professional image without creating a letterhead that is too busy (see page 108).

The reduced font size makes the letterhead work better: it has more authority. A sympathetic choice of typeface for the line 'United Reformed/Baptist Chapel' is used for visual relief. And the address for the church office is at the top. If the addresses of the ministers aren't needed, then a further, third layout using denominational logos can be created (see page 109).

There are many different ways to lay out a letterhead. The best way to work out what is right for your fellowship is to sketch some ideas on paper, using your corporate identity as a starting point. Look at letterheads you receive for inspiration,

think carefully about what will work and what won't in your situation. Encourage your designer to suggest some appropriate layouts. But don't clutter the letterhead with unnecessary information – keep it simple and to the point.

Adding denominational logos

If your church is affiliated to a Union, or wider church body, you might want to advertise this fact on your letterhead. Most Church organisations which encourage this make their logos available to download from their website. If in doubt, contact

the organisation directly. If you use a logo, ensure it is of the highest possible quality – if you have a version that fell off the back of the Internet, it will print poorly and reflect badly on the organisation in question.

Compliment slips

Compliment slips, usually a third of a sheet of A4, are a miniature version of the letterhead, only 'with compliments' is added and any superfluous details removed, such as

unnecessary addresses. My preferred size is A6 – you get four to a sheet (saving money) and still have enough space to write a short greeting on. Again, have these printed on a better quality paper, and never use a supply created by a photocopier or inkjet printer.

Business cards

Business cards are one of those great instant marketing tools people tend to hold on to them and they contain a person's contact details. Obviously they're a great tool for churches. But who needs them?

THE MINISTER

Attending conferences, meeting local residents, offering pastoral assistance: there are times when it's good to have some cards available to give out. Obviously, a minister must be comfortable with the information on the card: church address, home phone number, personal mobile and so on. If you value your days off, then don't give out your home number!

CHURCH OFFICERS

It's unlikely that they would need individually named cards, but having a supply of blank cards listing the contact details for the church office would be useful.

THE CHURCH MEMBERS

Not individually named cards, but a corporate church card is a useful marketing tool. For more details, see later in this chapter.

What makes a good business card?

The card must contain all the relevant information in a clearly structured hierarchy. If the text is all the same size, it is harder for the eye to work out what a card is saying. Compare the following examples, the first is set in the same size text, the second clearly structured.

The second card is easier to navigate: we know that Roger is the United Reformed minister of Collinstone Chapel and where to contact him – the manse would be the first place, the church office second.

Do you need to use colour?

The cards need to follow the letterhead's style. They are also used to leave a lasting impression of your church – so they need to be the best quality you can afford. It should use the colours in your corporate identity: that means using colour. Talk to your printer about this as they frequently offer stationery pack deals: letterheads, compliment slips and business cards for one price. Don't be tempted to cut corners and buy kits that feature sheets of thin perforated card which you can run through your inkjet printer – it is a false economy.

Collinstone Chapel
United Reformed / Baptist Chapel

Rev Roger Andrews
United Reformed minister

Manse:
123 Any Street, Collinstone, Rutland CZ1 2BC
Tel: (01234) 567890 rogerandrews@email.co.com

Church office:
Green Street, Collinstone, Rutland CZ1 2BC
(01234) 567890 collibcoffice@email.co.com

Collinstone Chapel
United Reformed / Baptist Chapel

Rev Roger Andrews
United Reformed minister

Manse:
123 Any Street, Collinstone, Rutland CZ1 2BC
Tel: (01234) 567890 rogerandrews@email.co.com

Church office:
Green Street, Collinstone, Rutland CZ1 2BC
(01234) 567890 collibcoffice@email.co.com

A card for the members

As explained earlier, it's helpful to offer a card for the members of the church to use when sharing the Gospel. This is something that we've tried in my home church: the idea is that people can use them to give to people when witnessing as it is something that would be kept. The front contains all the service information and contact details including the website,

Collinstone Chapel

United Reformed / Baptist Chapel

A warm welcome awaits you every Sunday!

10am   Morning worship with children's club
6.30pm   Evening worship

Green Street, Collinstone, Rutland CZ1 2BC
(01234) 567890 collibcoffice@email.co.com

www.collinstonechapel.co.uk

About Jesus

Jesus Christ is the most amazing person ever to have walked the Earth. He loved the 'losers', the 'strugglers', and the 'winners'. Today our lives can be changed by his death and rising again.

We have found that Jesus is not a made-up story, nor was he merely a wise teacher. He was either mad or telling the Truth.

Who do you think he is?

About the chapel

Collinstone Chapel is a group of people lovingly brought together by God. We're following him, trying to live out Jesus' teaching today in the village.

We take the Bible seriously and we're learning to live more in harmony with the Holy Spirit.

We hope you'll feel welcomed by real people whose lives have been touched by the real and loving God!

---

while the back has some blurb about the church and a short Gospel explanation. This text is only 130 words – just enough to get the salient points over without being too text heavy. They were handy for those that used them, but producing these requires a commitment among a fellowship to slip some into their purses and wallets and remember to hand them out at appropriate moments. Designed well, they will last two or three years.

Sending emails

Nearly everyone now uses email to keep in contact. It's an incredibly useful system for communicating (especially for sending out circulars from the pastor to the church members). Just as business letters are different from personal letters, email is a different process still: its immediate nature (mail usually arrives moments after it has been sent) means that it can be a more informal method of communication. But like a letter, it is up to the reader to infer the tone of the words. What might come across as a joke to you can be highly offensive to the recipient. Here are some tips to help you with your emails.

GET THE ADDRESS RIGHT

If an email needs to go to collinsbcoffice@email.co.com then that should be the address you type in. It's common for emails to be sent to the wrong person by mistake.

USE SUBJECT LINES

In an age where spam has become a byword for junk email, everyone hates having to remove pornographic emails from their system. You can help people pick out your emails by using clear subject lines: 'Thanks for help with Sunday's service' is better than 'Thank you', common in many junk emails.

DON'T USE CAPITALS

Just as you should never need to make an emphasis by underlining, you shouldn't use capitals to make a point in your emails. In Internet speak, it means you're ANGRY and you're SHOUTING to make your point.

REMEMBER IT'S A BUSINESS FORM OF COMMUNICATION

'Hi there! Hows it going?' might be fine for sending to someone you know well, but if you're emailing on church business, then you need to adopt business tones. 'Dear sir', etc. are still the order of the day.

DON'T USE FANCY GRAPHICS, TEXTS OR SPECIAL EFFECTS

You might like composing emails full of sound, pictures and flashing, colourful letters, but it sends out a signal about your fellowship and can be confused with junk emails. Stick to plain text with no formatting – your recipient will receive smaller emails and they can adjust the text size accordingly.

WATCH YOUR ATTACHMENTS

Sending picture files, amusing Internet jokes and sound clips are all very well, but you should ask the recipient whether they want it or not first. If they have a dial-up connection, they will not thank you for wasting their phone bill so they can download a 4MB file that contains pictures of cute kittens. Send the smallest possible file size you can: if a word processing document has images in them, compress them. If you're sending a photo, use image editing software to reduce the file size so it's about 50k. Likewise, attachments can contain viruses so ensure that your email is virus checked before leaving your computer. And if you're sending out a circular email to a large number of people, don't send graphics: it is more likely to get rejected as spam as they will count the number of addresses that the email is being sent to.

CHECK IT BEFORE SENDING

No one is a perfect typist – mistakes can be made all the time. If it's important, you might want to ask someone else to proofread your email first. But never send an email without checking it over. You might have thought you'd typed 'I don't want 50,000 doughnuts delivered to the church' but you could have typed 'I do want ... ' Look out also for things that could backfire, especially if you are responding in an emotional way to an email. Beware of humorous asides that could be misconstrued, anger that will make a delicate situation worse or double entendres that aren't meant to be there.

BE PATIENT

Although emails arrive instantly, there might be a myriad of reasons as to why you don't get a prompt response. The recipient might not be at their computer, they might be prioritising other work, or they might even have decided that no action needs to be taken. Some emails do go astray, so if you want to be sure that yours has been received, tick the box on your email composing software to 'send receipt'. When the email is opened and read, the recipient will be asked if they want to send you an acknowledgement: you will then know that your email has been received.

TEN

THE BIG ONES:
PLANNING FOR CHRISTMAS
AND EASTER

Christmas and Easter are the two occasions in the Church year when attendance rises. We might be a nation of Christmas shoppers (£15.4 billion spent in 2004), but we still want to acknowledge the new born/risen King at appropriate moments. A Church of England survey before a recent Christmas revealed that 43 per cent of the population were planning to go to a church service at Christmas; not necessarily Christmas Day, but possibly a carol, watchnight or Christingle service. Out of the entire Church year, these are the services that matter the most. Getting them wrong is not an option, so planning for them must start early.

In January, review your Christmas services

Invite church members to offer feedback from visitors, friends or even themselves. Were the services too long? Did they like the music? Where they uncomfortable with sharing the peace? Was there too much jargon? Mulled wine not up to much? Cover all aspects of the services. After letting the church council discuss the feedback, write a report to help with planning for the forthcoming services.

Thank God for the opportunity you had to share the Good News with visitors, and pray that the Holy Spirit will touch their lives. Pray for wisdom in planning the forthcoming Christmas services, that the Holy Spirit will help guide the decisions made later in the year.

If running a Lent course

Start promoting the course no later than four weeks before Lent starts, to give enough notice for people to block out the appropriate time and buy appropriate materials. You could launch the Lent course with a pancake party in the church hall, including a short talk introducing the theme; this should also attract the attention of the local media looking for Pancake Day stories. If the course is open to non-churchgoers, then ensure that Easter services are promoted at the sessions – let the course be a build-up to Easter Day.

Work out the pattern for your Easter weekend

First, determine what resources are available as there is little point in planning a fantastic Passion Play if half your congregation treat the long Easter weekend as an ideal time to go away. Is there a Maundy Thursday service? A Good Friday walk of witness? An Easter breakfast or an Easter egg hunt? Decide what, as a fellowship, you are capable of. Ensure that the church is spring-cleaned before the first service, so it looks its best: it should sparkle. Let the local media know what is happening and when, so that the events can be publicised. A press release should include a quote from a pastor saying why Easter is so important; see chapter 13 for help with this.

Be a welcoming church

Think about how churches are decorated for weddings and adapt some of the flourishes that will add to the atmosphere: a warm welcome, flowers, ribbons, hot cross buns or mini eggs after the service, balloons, new banners, the best worship band/organist your church can muster, etc. Easter is an exciting celebration, so it should be treated as such. Encourage members of the congregation to invite friends and family to the service.

Run a seeker course straight after Easter

Alpha recommends a rolling programme, offering at least three courses a year. If newcomers worship at Easter, they should have an opportunity to ask the questions they want the answers to. A course like *Alpha* or *Christianity Explored* will give them that opportunity. Similarly, run a course in the New Year and promote it heavily at your Christmas services. If you feel that you haven't got the resources to run a course, then consider other evangelistic events such as a 'grill a Christian' evening.

After Easter services, hold a review

Carry out a similar review to that of your Christmas services, as this is the best way to learn how to put on a better 'show' the following year. Welcome all criticism, but don't take it personally.

Set the dates for the Christmas services before the summer holidays start

Do this in June so the people who are leading parts of the service can block time off in their diaries and spend part of the summer thinking about the choices they need to make: drama, carols, etc.

Start planning seriously for Christmas in September

With everyone back from the summer holidays, people will be ready to start the marathon to Advent. If the service is to be spectacular, then it needs to be planned properly; if the church is forming an orchestra or choir, then the pieces need to be practised and essentials such as catering needs to be worked out. Announce the plans and themes at a church members' meeting. This lets everyone feel involved and reinforces the importance of the services.

Start practising from September

The more rehearsal time the more polished the end result. This requires the leaders and conductors to be organised and start arranging their elements of the service early; if the service requirements haven't been set in stone, use the first rehearsals as a bonding time. Starting early gives the luxury of time, useful for improving performances; you won't get this if you start rehearsing at the end of November.

Have the formats finalised by October half-term

The organiser of the services (and probably the speaker too) will need to have everything worked out by the end of October:

the readings, the carols, the order of the service – giving enough time to find appropriate people for each job.

Design the publicity materials in October

If you are to maximise the attendance at your church's Christmas services, the local community needs to be invited. It is worth spending money on a leaflet delivered to every house in the neighbourhood. Don't wait until early November to think about cobbling something together – especially if you can share production costs and delivery chores with other churches in your area. Working together will enable you to spend less to get a better result. My church has joined with others for the past few years, and has produced a full-colour Christmas card costing each church about two hundred pounds each for several thousand copies; it would have cost each church four times that to produce the same thing individually. A case study on the latest card follows. To work out when they need to be finished by, work backwards from the distribution date. Usually, this is the end of the second week in December, so you need to allow two Sundays for them to be collected and delivered.

It is vital that the publicity looks professional; if you only spend money on publicity once a year this is the time to do it, and the treasurer should earmark appropriate funds to do so. Go for the best you can afford, order from companies such as CPO (www.cpo.org.uk), design your own or employ someone to design them. Ensure they are printed on thick card and not thin paper (a minimum paper weight of 160gsm, preferably 250gsm) – paper will crease and tear as it is delivered through letterboxes. Under no circumstances be prepared to cut corners and produce a black and white photocopied or risographed sheet of day-glo paper: these look cheap and (in this context) nasty. One example I've seen is an A5 sheet folded to make an A6 four-page leaflet: the front featured a child's drawing of a star with a Bible quote about the wise men following the star in a children's handwriting font. It did not say 'come to church': it said 'we're cheapskates'.

Make sure that the information printed inside is clear and uses the minimum of text. Stick to a short introduction about Christmas (no more than 30 words), a greeting and the service times. Keep the language simple, don't be tempted to use 'thees', 'thous' and 'wherefores' (remember not everyone has English as a first language, and research suggests that not everyone has an adult reading age) and ensure that the message is welcoming. Avoid phrases that make you sound like a killjoy, so no 'it's not just parties, booze and presents' because you'll be judging a lot of unchurched people who celebrate Christmas like that. If you live in an area where a large ethnic community exists – a Chinese, Greek or Hindu community for example – find someone who speaks the language and can add a Christmas greeting in the appropriate script. It's a little touch that shows that God's love is for everyone, not just those who can read English.

Make clear which services are particularly aimed at children (family carol service, toddler's Christmas celebration, etc.) and check that all the dates are correct. Use Christmas Eve and Christmas Day, rather than December 24 and 25. Ensure the times are correct – no watchnight Christmas Eve services at 11.30 a.m. – and the correct times are noon and midnight, not the ambiguous 12 p.m. and 12 a.m. If you're holding a candlelight service and need people to bring torches, then say so. Likewise, if a service is outdoors, then make it clear that people will need to wrap up warm.

Approach volunteers from November

For these services, you need the best members on hand to welcome people as they enter and leave the church; ensure that the people organising the post-service catering are efficient and will not panic if five hundred guests descend on them. Ensure that the stewards know their way around the church and will be able to cope with problems during the service. Ask the best sound technician and video desk operators to be on duty so that everyone can hear and see the service. Find the florist who can produce appropriate displays. Ensure that the church is decorated with appropriate Christmas decorations. Cover every aspect of the service and approach individuals; getting people to volunteer is often like trying to herd cats.

Deliver the leaflets early in December

You can pay Royal Mail to deliver leaflets for you, but the service has restrictions: a minimum quantity of 9,500 homes, you have to fall within the right sector (so this might not reach everyone in your neighbourhood if the postcode areas change) and they will only accept bookings up to the first week in December. Expect a mail drop to 10,000 homes to cost about five hundred pounds. Your local free newspaper can deliver them inside its pages; the disadvantage of this is that some households throw the paper away without even opening it. Prices will vary from paper to paper.

The most cost-effective way is to get members of the church to deliver them. It will take some office time to collate them into appropriate piles corresponding to streets, but it will cost significantly less and is a ministry that most in the church can feel part of, especially those who feel uncomfortable with face-to-face evangelism.

If the church delivers the Christmas leaflets, follow the delivery code

Every week I receive about a dozen different takeaway menus: pizzas, curries, Chinese and more pizzas. Most are left sticking out of the letterbox, all are thrown straight into the recycling bin. Instead of being welcome, they're a nuisance. Likewise, my two free newspapers are delivered, rain or shine, by willing paper boys and girls – but the paper is rarely pushed all the way through the letterbox. This is a signal to any would-be burglars that I'm out so it's an ideal time to let themselves in.

When we're guests we have to be on best behaviour, and this extends to delivering leaflets. This might seem pedantic but we have to give good impressions of our churches.

- If you have to open a gate, close it on the way out

- If the sign says 'no leaflets or free newspapers' then respect their wishes

- Always push the leaflet all the way through the letterbox; don't leave anything sticking out, no matter how awkward the letterbox

- Don't be nosy and look to see if people are in/what their houses are like

- Don't deliver early in the morning or late at night; letterboxes clatter and can wake people/scare nervous residents

- If you see people, greet them with a smile and wish them a happy Christmas. Remember that even delivering leaflets about church services is an important act of witness.

Let the local media know about the services, especially any unusual activities

Let them know three weeks in advance of your first service what is happening and suggest possible picture opportunities: a children's nativity, a Christingle service, carol singers with lanterns, live animals and so on. Ensure that you give daytime contact details so that follow-up questions can be arranged. If the newspaper can't send a photographer, find someone in the fellowship with a good quality digital camera and send out a press release containing appropriate pictures no later than 24 hours after the relevant event. For more on this, see chapter 13.

Get the church praying

Commit these services to God – after all, they're designed to enable non-regular attendees worship him. Ask people in the fellowship to pray as you prepare, to pray as people rehearse, to pray before the services for the people attending, during that the Holy Spirit will touch people's lives, and afterwards, that friendships made on the night will encourage guests to come to faith.

Practise, practise, practise

Comprehensive advice on how to plan and deliver effective outreach services is beyond the scope of this book, but everything about these services must live up to the quality of the publicity. If you have drama and music, these will have been worked on from September. Practise the changeovers between parts of the service, as it needs to be slick and professional. People reading Bible passages need to know when to come to the front. They must know where to stand, how to position the microphone so that they can be heard clearly and have their Bibles ready. Those responsible for the sound system need to know in advance which parts of the service will need to be amplified and sent to the hearing-aid loop system. The preacher must also know where to stand so they can be seen and heard by everyone. If you have an orchestra or choir, then practise their entrances and exits, work out where the best places are to seat them in the church. Check and double check all computer equipment, slides and service sheets; ask people to proofread them.

If you want a donkey ...

Book as early as you can. There are many farms that offer donkey hire (or other livestock if you want sheep or goats), but donkey hire is popular. If you leave it to the last minute, then you run the risk of being disappointed. As soon as you decide you want livestock (perhaps at your first planning meeting) get on the phone and book.

Case study: east Reading churches Christmas leaflet 2005

The brief

To produce a leaflet to go through 8,000 doors in east Reading to advertise services celebrating Christmas taking place in the neighbourhood's four churches.

The background

The churches had worked together to produce a Christmas leaflet for several years. This approach sends out a message to the community: 'we might be different, but we're united by the Gospel.' It means we can target more homes as the churches share the same catchment area and share delivery chores. Finally, working together gives an economy of scale as there is more money available to spend on the leaflet.

The 2002 leaflet was A6 sized, with a colour front and a black and white reverse printed on 140gsm paper (almost thin card). It wasn't successful as there was more text than space. In 2003, material from CPO was used to tie in with *The Lord of the Rings*. In 2004, the decision was made to switch to A5, this time full colour on both sides on 100gsm thinner paper – as a cost-saving measure. This false economy was made apparent when the paper buckled during deliveries.

The other complaint from the 2004 leaflet was that it looked like a pizza leaflet. The theme was, 'Would it still be Christmas without Jesus?' and asked if it would be Christmas without trees, cards, crackers or snow, pointing out that they are either modern inventions or rare. Illustrated with garish colours, some traditional church people didn't like it and wanted something more appropriate in 2005. A nativity scene was suggested.

Solving the problem of size and the weight of the paper was the priority: churches need to budget for the most cost-effective solution. After discussing the idea with my local printer, we found a range of A6 Christmas cards, full colour on both sides, but twice the 2004 price. A card that could stand on a mantelpiece was hard to turn down. It also meant that we had four sides to play with (the card is A5 folded to A6) so the service times could have the right amount of space and a suitable mini-sermon or Christmas message could be added.

Full colour enables the churches to attract people's attention and look professional.

The planning

Once the date and the theme for the main carol service had been set, we then had to work backwards. While most of the events were taking place on Sunday 18 December, there were a few held on 11 December. This meant that the cards needed to be distributed in advance of that day – supplies needed to be available no later than 4 December. We built in an extra week just in case something went wrong: so the cards had to come back from the printers on Friday 25 November. Past experience has taught me to build a couple of days grace on to that – so that was Wednesday 23 November.

Having set the finish date, it was a case of then working back from that again – how long did the printers need? In this case, it was 10 business days. That gave three weeks to design something that everyone would be happy with, and for church ministers and pastors to finalise their service times.

A starting point

Here's the initial e-mail for the theme:

> Here are my first thoughts for Christmas. Let me know what you think.
>
> The theme is likely to be something on 'light shining in the darkness'.
>
> We need to be praying. Probably more visitors to Church over Christmas than in the rest of the year combined.

The starting point was light. The first thing to do was to think creatively: Christmas lights, stars, Jesus as the light of the world, candle light, fairy lights, street and tree decorations. One train of thought was that Jesus is God's gift: what if we took a picture of someone opening a present only to find that the box contained light? It would have been hard to get right, but it could have been done by wrapping up a cardboard box leaving the flaps at the top open and then cutting out the bottom so that a desk lamp or a powerful halogen light could have been placed inside. Taken against a dark background, we could have created the illusion that the box contained the gift of light. It was a nice idea, but a little complicated for the time available.

One church offered their suggestions too:

My own thoughts are that, particularly if we are going to do a Christmas card a religious one might be nice. I realise your message is religious but people will only read it once if at all. The picture is what they will remember and may display.

A nativity scene would be more unusual, stand out more, could be made to fit in with the theme of light in darkness and, if clever, could give echoes of Kashmir and other problems more serious than Christmas ties. Most men solve that one by buying themselves a bottle of whiskey. Most women solve the problem of buying presents in the same way. What we are 'selling' is Jesus not the tedium of a secular Christmas. Most people actually like Christmas. One of my daughters has still not forgiven the Church for a vicar she thought was saying we shouldn't have Christmas presents. This is the world's perception of us!

Someone else suggested:

```
Why not an astronomical picture for 'light shining
in the darkness'? One of the many planetary
nebulae - in colour would be stunning
```

Pictures of the galaxies, look like blobs from a distance, so they don't have that wow factor you need when people pick up a card from their doormat. It would also have to be bought from a photographic agency.

Initial ideas

The only way to start working out what would work on a card was to doodle. So, I did some sketches, trying to visualise what would work.

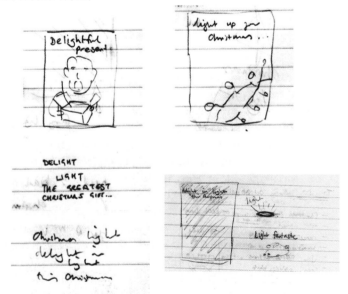

I wanted to work first on a slogan – light shining in the darkness would mean nothing to a non-church goer. They might have some dim memory of their old Sunday School teacher giving a talk on Jesus' words about not hiding a light under a bushel – but what's a bushel? The moment people ask questions about a slogan, it stops working. As the slogan was also going on the front of the card, people needed a reason to turn inside. It needed to be a question or affirmative statement of some kind. That ruled out 'Why not come to church?' as it's a vague non-assertive question. If people can answer 'No' to a question, then don't ask it.

I played around with some concepts, including delight, Christmas light, Christmas gifts ... and also tried to work out what people associate with light at Christmas.

Being of that generation, I remembered a Spice Girls song 'Spice Up Your Life', which could be altered – Light up your life. That didn't have a festive connection. What about 'Light up your life this Christmas'? Too long. 'Light up your Christmas': it allows some interchange between the slogan and the picture.

First draft

While the initial thoughts of light shining out of a box were quickly dismissed as technically difficult to achieve in a short timescale, I did like the idea of light coming out of the darkness. That gave two clear ideas: a Christmas star, as most people are aware that the Magi followed the star; or a string of festive fairy lights, twinkling away and glowing with energy. The doodles looked promising – but how do you make a star look like it's full of life? One possible way was to create one on the computer, but it would somehow seem fake.

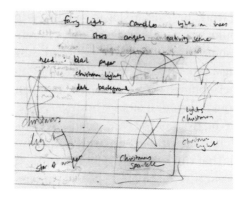

The eureka moment came after looking at the date: we were, at that time, close to the firework season. Children enjoy writing their names in sparklers. Using a slow shutter speed on a camera, it would be possible to draw a five-pointed star with a sparkler. The fairy light idea also needed to be tested as it is festive, lending itself to a Christmas card.

So, to ensure that the ideas worked, and to get feedback from the fellowships involved, a first draft was produced, sourcing suitable images found from a Google search to give a proper flavour of each idea.

Feedback from the churches gave the star a seal of approval. However, one comment swung it for the star: 'I like the sparkler star best. The other looks a little like one of those pictures taken close up or at an odd angle so that you have to guess what it is.' A star is a star is a star – it's one of those shapes that we draw as children and know that it's a star.

Photography

Of course, we couldn't have taken a picture from the Internet without permission – that's a breach of copyright and not very ethical. Churches have to be above reproach in their business transactions. So, we took our own photo. The idea was tried out with an LED light to ensure it would work.

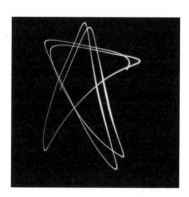

Confident it did, we lit a sparkler and snapped away. Almost 40 different star pictures were taken (one reject is shown) to get the right one. The main expense for producing this picture was 99 pence for a packet of sparklers.

Using image editing software, we removed both the background from the star and me, so that all we had was the cut-out sparkler star so it could be placed onto a solid blue background. This second proof was then circulated among the churches.

Making changes

With the image approved, it was time to turn the attention to the text on the card. Some people suggested the typeface for the service times was too small. A third draft was produced adjusting this, but it was still considered to be imperfect. When you're designing something and ask for feedback, people need to give you honest criticism. Because it's a creative process, it's hard to step back and listen to their comments as you have a sense of ownership of your work. By taking these comments on board it made the end result better. As space was limited, the only thing that could be changed was switching to a typeface with a larger x-height (for an explanation, see chapter 2). New Century Schoolbook fitted the bill in this case, as it looks a lot larger than it is, which is why it's been used extensively in newspapers.

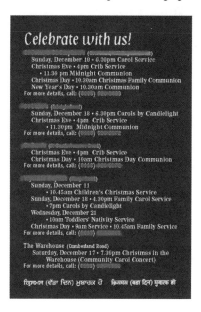

Final changes

One thing that I wasn't happy with but no one else had noticed, was the slogan 'Light up your Christmas' – it lacked energy compared with the picture of the star, looking rather comical and poor. However, by taking the lettering into a photo manipulation programme, it was possible to add in some special effects, giving it a glow that made it three-dimensional and full of life, just like the star.

The distribution

Each church was allocated a section of the community to which to deliver the cards. Volunteers were ready to sort out the cards into piles for different streets, according to a street map containing the number of houses in each road. The cards came back from the printers scored, not folded: another job for the volunteers. It was decided not to place the cards into an envelope, partly due to cost but mainly because we needed people to pick up the card from the doormat and say 'Wow!' when they saw it.

The poster

To tie in with the cards, my church requested a poster to go outside the church, advertising only its own services but in keeping with the theme. This was straightforward to do, and adapted the format of the poster, placing the star on the left and the minimum amount of text on the right. It cost another £65 to produce and was stunning.

Christmas and Easter are the best witness opportunities that churches ever get; hopefully this chapter has inspired you to make the most of these two festivals in your community.

ELEVEN

FOOTBALL, EUROVISION OR POP IDOL? EVENTS ON THE BIG SCREEN

Every so often, our nations go football crazy: everyone crams round a big screen to catch the latest match. A staggering 20.7 million viewers watched the England v Argentina game during the 2002 World Cup. That's not including the people who were in pubs and clubs, which were full to bursting. Football still brings us together.

England's opening game in the World Cup of 2002 fell on the Sunday morning of the Queen's Golden Jubilee: a long bank holiday of celebrations. Naturally, some churches made use of this and, instead of holding the usual morning service, threw hugely popular parties. As well as offering a big screen, churches can provide a safe, family-friendly environment, with face painting, music, games, food and an alcohol-free space.

So, it's worth making the most of these occasions – and others like them, such as the Eurovision Song Contest and even the finale of shows like *Pop Idol* or *Doctor Who*. These are events where the church can show that it is in touch with the world around it, offer some extras and reach out to people who wouldn't normally go to church. It also celebrates the family, something that pubs can't do.

World Cup or European games that affect the home nations (England, Wales, Scotland, Northern Ireland and Ireland) occasionally clash with church services. Some people think that service times are sacrosanct and should never be moved, especially as football can be a false idol. It's worth moving a service time if it brings in people who only usually come to church for weddings, christenings and funerals: it's one of the easiest forms of outreach you can ever do. Hold a short service half an hour before the programme starts; give God the glory and make it clear that the church doesn't worship football, but enjoys watching it from time to time. Remember that there's nothing in the Bible about the times that services should be held. In 2002, the then Archbishop of Canterbury, Dr George Carey, told BBC News: 'Worship comes first of course, but the World Cup only comes round every four years, so we can afford to be flexible.'

Legal obligations

How you choose to organise the screening is up to you but there are legal obligations you'll need to fulfil, notably with your licence. We also have a moral obligation to ensure that what we do is above board: the last thing we need is 'church fined over lack of TV licence' scandals.

If a church has a TV or video onsite that can receive TV signals, then it must have a licence specific to the church buildings. For more details, log on to The TV Licensing website: www.tvlicensing.co.uk or call (0870) 241 5590.

There are some other caveats: if you broadcast a game, you must show the credits. You cannot superimpose your own messages onto the screen, such as 'hot dogs available now' or imply that your church is one of the match sponsors or is associated with the broadcaster. Under no circumstances should you charge admission or ask for donations in lieu of admission. In 2002, some churches did and were prosecuted by FIFA for doing so. You can charge for refreshments and sundry activities as long as there is no association with the World Cup branding.

You might also want to show matches from Sky – Sunday afternoon bring and share lunch with football? The satellite organisation offers a range of subscription packages. A spokesperson said, 'Church properties that sell alcohol or charge an admission fee would go on a general contract with a monthly subscription from [currently] £210 per month + VAT.'

However, if your church doesn't sell alcohol, or charge an admission fee, you can get it much cheaper: the concessionary rate for public viewing on a general contract is currently £51 per month + VAT.

Unlike the licence fee arrangement, Sky will allow you to ask for donations in lieu of an admission fee. For details, log on to: business.sky.com/general_packages.asp.

Ensure you know the maximum number of people that health and safety regulations will permit to be in your church hall and you have the right insurance.

Equipment needed

The first thing you'll need will be a data projector, which will cost you about five hundred pounds, essential for the big picture. Position it in the room so that the screen will be seen by everyone – and then think about how much cable and so on you'll need to get from the TV aerial to the big screen.

The aerial will also need a tuner. This could be a small portable television, but you'll need to ensure that this can be connected to the data projector. I've used a video recorder in the past: connecting the aerial into it, and then connected the data projector via a Scart lead. The projected image was then used to tune in the video to get the picture. This was much easier than lugging a TV around. You could also use a computer that has a TV Tuner card, but only use a machine that is reliable: if it crashes just before a winning goal, you will face a mutiny.

The sound came from speakers that were also plugged into the video; ideal for the dozen or so of us that gathered for Eurovision, but it probably won't be right for the crowd watching a football game. You will also need to think about whether you'll need a microphone to announce anything during the game. Talk to your church's sound operator and find out what they recommend: it's impossible to give anything other than generic advice because every church is different.

Make sure that you test the proposed system, however much a lash-up, at least a week before the day of the event. Absolutely nothing must go wrong with the sound and the picture on the day.

Plan the event

The easiest thing to do, especially if it's a football game on a sunny Saturday afternoon, is to show the game and offer some refreshments at half-time and after the final whistle, everyone goes home. But you can arrange for other entertainment to encourage people to feel comfortable and relaxed spending time in a Christian environment. Think of events that are suitable for your target audience: face painting, a 'beat the goalie' competition, a five-a-side mini-tournament, a disco or live band, church fête-type side shows.

Are you going to tie everything together with a prologue or an epilogue? Who can deliver a suitable message, keeping it short and entertaining? Will you make available Christian tracts and literature for people to take away afterwards?

If you're going to offer food, then think about the type of people who will be there: if you live in an area with a large Muslim or Jewish community then find appropriate halal, kosher or vegetarian food and cook it accordingly.

If in doubt, keep it simple. Open the venue an hour before kick-off, have some low-key music in the background and offer some soft drinks. About 20 minutes before the game, have a 5 to 10-minute welcome talk, detailing various practicalities that could be segued into a short Gospel appeal. Then let the match build-up begin. During half-time offer hot dogs and drinks. After the match, people will be emotionally affected by what they saw, be it a good or bad result; this is possibly the worst time to offer any preaching, so let people drift away of their own accord or offer additional entertainment.

If you're hosting a Eurovision party, remember it's a May Saturday night (with a late finish) so people will want snacks (crisps, nuts, etc.), seats and tables. You can offer scorecards, make it fancy dress, invite people to bring cheese and have fun.

Advertise the event wisely

You must decide what is best for your church: an invitation to the whole community, or a closed event which church members invite their friends and work colleagues along to.

What you decide will depend on how comfortable you are in arranging these types of events, as an open event could attract the world and their dog. But flag up the family-friendliness of the event: children are welcome, parents are welcome and men are welcome. Ensure that the terms and conditions are known: be upfront about a no-alcohol rule (or allow people to bring their own), or a request for donations for refreshments.

If you decide to make it an open event, let your local media know: send them a press release in good time. Prepare a picture to send to the papers: perhaps one of the church's pastors blowing a referee's whistle while another church member holds a football. Only allow yourselves to be draped in the appropriate national flag if you are comfortable with this. In areas where racism is rife, it may send out the wrong signal to people. In the run-up to a major football tournament, every newspaper wants to run football stories: this fits the bill. Prepare posters and ask your local shops to put them in their windows, and let the congregation pass round the flyers. Alternatively, for the low-key approach tell the fellowship and get them to offer personal invitations.

Let the neighbours know

If you're going to be noisy (and when you celebrate a goal, you make noise) then be courteous and warn your neighbours – invite them along, let them know what time the event is likely to end.

Get the right amount of help

Volunteers will be needed to set the halls up, especially if you need chairs and tables. Audio-visual experts will be needed to ensure the game can be seen. Cooks and servers will need to be around to help with the refreshments and you'll need people prepared to clean up the mess afterwards.

Decorate the hall

Get the bunting out! Put up wallcharts, posters and pictures: anything that will help create an atmosphere and make people feel welcome. Also think about where you're going to put any Christian literature or information about groups that the church runs – on the tables where people are sitting? By the doorway? By the serving hatch? And make sure that the material is relevant to the event you're hosting. For a football match, anticipate a lot of dads coming along, so let them know if you run a football team that needs players, a dad and toddler group, a curry club, a men's group. Likewise, list your youth events and make them sound like fun rather than torture.

Have fun

If you set everything up properly and have arranged enough volunteers then you'll have the opportunity to enjoy the event yourself. Make the most of witness opportunities like this, and go for it.

TWELVE

BEING NET-SAVVY: THE INTERNET

Is the Internet still an undiscovered country for your church? Or, did some kind soul knock up something a few years ago, but no one has known how to update it since? Maybe you just think that you don't need a website, as people will come to church regardless. A website should provide information that will help would-be visitors look round the church to suss out if it's the kind of place that they would want to go to. It provides an immediate contact point for your community. If you think that your church doesn't need a website, think again. Gordon Thorn, from Christian website builder www.Church123.com says of his church, 'We get one or two visitors – both Christians moving to the area and seekers – every week. Our website is our number one outreach tool.' Your church's website is a vital resource for introducing people to the Gospel. It can also be a great resource for your church members, so you have to work out the right kind of site for your situation.

There can also be no excuse for slapping together a simple page that has your church name, address and contact details (plus a large photograph that takes ages to download of the church pictured through fuzzy rain with several fast cars going past). 'A bad church website may stop people from ever visiting the church and may reinforce the stereotype that the church is out of touch and irrelevant,' says Gordon. 'If you are going to have a website you must resolve to have a good one! A church website is an on-going commitment, not a one-off project to enable you to tick a box saying "website done."'

Have you ever looked at websites designed by churches? The standards vary enormously. Some are very slick, put together by volunteers who enjoy their hobby. Others are good sites easily created using online web building systems. And there are also lots of church sites that were made several years ago when the Internet was in its infancy and haven't been updated since; they look amateurish, with little thought put into either content or design. If your site looks poor and is out of date, remove it and start again. If you don't know how to take it down, then contact one of the Christian website builders.

Aim your site at both Christians and non-Christians

When designing a site, do some research. Look at the websites that you enjoy visiting and see how they structure themselves. Without exception, websites are divided into pages, each one addressing a different topic. Translated to a church website, this means you can offer two different areas on your site: one for visitors and one for church members.

'The church website offers potential visitors an ideal way to find out about your church, and the Christian faith, in an anonymous way before taking the plunge and coming along in person. Your site needs to be accessible in language and style giving these visitors a positive impression,' says Gordon. This means that on the general information pages you must avoid jargon at all costs, especially when people don't know their Pentecost from their St Swithin's Day. Be visitor-friendly and, if in doubt, check your site with a non-Christian friend before it goes up for the whole world to see. If they don't understand something, then the wording needs changing.

Making the site a resource for church members is also important. The most obvious way is to let members download sermon or housegroup notes and list details of that weekend's services and rotas. Some churches offer a password-protected area which includes a forum (a discussion board). This is great as it allows space for points from sermons to be debated, a book group to be set up and pleas for help.

Always remember that a website gives a snapshot of what your fellowship is like – don't let the world see documents or information that could give a negative impression of the church – so no minutes of difficult church meetings, financial reports etc.

What should a website contain?

The first thing to do when planning a church website is to decide on the content: it's easy to create lots of all-singing all-dancing graphics, but unless you actually make the right information readily available, people will leave the site. What do you want people to know? The least you should include is the church's name, contact details, the address and when the church meets. But there are other ideas you can incorporate:

The home page

This is the first page that any visitor will see, hence the name. Think of it as the front page *and* a contents page. Look at various homepages of other websites to get an idea.

Visitors

Include a page that outlines to visitors what to expect. This can cover anything from where to park and what to wear to how long services last and whether you have accessible facilities. See www.thekingschurch.com (then click Visitors) for a good example.

The kind of questions that visitors ask will include:

- Is this church weird, or do normal people go as well?
- What do Christians believe? Why do people go to church?
- Where is the church? How do I get in contact?
- What times are the services? Which service should I go to?
- What events/activities are they running that interest me?
- Are there facilities for children?

Church services

A list of when and where the church meets. If you update the site regularly, you can add in the sermon themes and the speaker's details. It's also helpful to include a guide to car parking for people visiting your services.

Special services

Details of how to contact the church if you want to get married; have your child christened or blessed; or need to arrange a funeral.

The church leaders

Not just who is the church's priest, vicar, minister or pastor (and how to contact them), but who serves on the parish council or diaconate – and what their brief is. Do not include home addresses, especially for those with financial responsibility.

Real life stories

It's great to include some testimonies on the site. Have a few from different people appealing to a range of visitors. Ensure they are written in plain English and not Christian jargon.

The ethos behind the church

What is the church's vision and mission? What kind of church are you? This page is your main selling space, as people will make their formal judgments about you according to what they read here. If you are a denominational church, then you can explain a little about its structure and beliefs.

Activities within the church

If you have groups meeting during the week, then you can list them as an A–Z or in day order, including a description of what the activity is and how to join up.

Youth and children's activities

What is there for young people? Scouts? Girls' Brigade? Something else? Use your site to let people know about the various activities that they can join in with. Get the young people involved in the creation of these pages. As part of your child protection never include pictures of minors without written permission from the carer and never include children's names or contact details on the website.

A history of the church

Let people know how long you have been in 'business' for, any moves, pastoral staff, missions, growth, revivals. Make it good news – remember most people are interested in people rather than buildings.

Contact us

Any website worth its salt offers contact details, usually via an email form (to help prevent your email address being used to send spam or flooded with junk emails). Ensure that this includes the full address of the church, a contact phone number for the church office and a link to a street map website, such as multimap.co.uk or streetmap.co.uk. You can also suggest that people send in their prayer needs.

The church newsletter

It's possible to upload the pages from your church newsletter to the site, but be sure to edit out anything that is for church members only.

Sermon notes

Pastors can offer their notes after the service, and readings and themes before the service to help people prepare.

Feel free to explore other ideas for websites and ignore some of the suggestions above if they aren't appropriate for your situation. Once you've created your basic list of pages count how many there are. If you have 12 or less then you can stick to simple navigation (all pages visible on the main menu). If you have too many pages on the main menu it will become cluttered and difficult to use. If there are more than 12, then you will need to consider grouping the pages. For example if you have four different youth groups (by age) then you can have one page on the main menu called Youth – clicking on the Youth page opens up an introductory page with general information and provides links out to a sub page for each group. Keep navigation simple and include the main menu on every page.

What not to contain

The strength of the Internet is that your webpage is visible to whole world. So as you go to bed after uploading the church's website, someone on the other side of the world can be downloading that week's sermon notes. It's a great way to keep in touch, especially if you want to offer (stream) sermons for people to listen to as if it were a radio station. Your missionaries could benefit from this as they could still take part in the church's teaching programme, view pictures from the church's Christmas party or find out the latest news of the fellowship. The downside to all this is that your missionaries could actually be working in a part of the world where it is not safe for their presence to be advertised. So be very sensitive about the information that you put on the website.

Here are some points to be aware of:

Be careful about giving out personal details for church members

Placing home addresses is an invitation for burglars to pay a visit while the occupants are at church. This is especially true of any church officers who take money home from services to bank on Monday. Seek permission from parents of any children featured on the site. Some may not be comfortable with their child appearing for all and sundry to see.

Be sensitive to the work carried out by your missionaries

Anyone in the world can read your website, and they might not be sympathetic to the Christian faith.

Watch the language that you use ...

With the Internet allowing you to publish anything, it's tempting to say whatever you want – but an ungracious choice of language can make your church appear to be bigoted, or conforming to the stereotypes. Be life-affirming, not soul-destroying.

Watch out for jargon in your Statement of Faith

It might make sense to members of your denomination, but the chances are it won't to non-Christians. On your 'what we believe' page, use this statement as a starting point and rewrite it to be easily understandable. One church's web-friendly 'about us' statement is as follows:

'We are a group of ordinary people called together by a loving God. He sent his Son, Jesus Christ, to live in this world, to die in our place, and to rise from the dead; we're now following him, trying to live out the truth of the Bible, in the 21st century, in our community. We are over 500 adults from all races and backgrounds (with the largest age group being the thirty-and twenty-somethings) plus about 200 children. Two-thirds of us live within one mile of the church building. We meet to worship on Sundays, in homes midweek for closer friendship, and at other times too many to mention, for (among other things) fun. We take the Bible seriously and we try to make the Christian faith understandable to everyone. We hope that whatever contact you have with us, through this website or by actually dropping in, you'll feel welcomed by people who live in the real world and whose lives have been touched by the real and loving God!'

People should hopefully be able to identify with this far more than 'We believe in one God ...' approach. Although this is true, it won't necessarily draw people to your fellowship.

Don't start with a history of your church

Collinstone Community Church's building might have been erected in 1934, but it is the people who make the church, not the bricks. People relate to people far more than they relate to buildings, unless the building is of significant architectural interest.

Out of date news

A website is for life, but the content isn't. Think about the message yours sends out if it still has pictures on from church activities that took place four years ago. Either create a site that needs little updating or design one that can be updated with ease. It is for these situations that an online web building package comes into its own.

Choose a good name

The address (domain name) for your website is very important. It should clearly identify your church and be memorable, the shorter the better, as you need to type this into your Internet programme to access the site. If your Internet service provider (ISP) offers webspace, then your basic web address could be something long and complicated like: http://homepage.Your ISPsName.com/judithmary/collinstonechurch/Homepage.htm. You'd give any visitor repetitive strain injury typing that address in. Buying a memorable domain name is much easier. Instead of that mouthful, you could choose www.collinstonecommun itychurch.co.uk or www.collinstonechristians.co.uk. Produce a shortlist of possible domain names and check to see if they are available, using a website such as www.123-reg.co.uk. You will pay a yearly fee to own a domain name, and it will be registered as yours with Nominet. If you need advice, ask some of the Christian web-building companies for advice.

How do we build a website?

There are three main ways to build a website:

Use a web-building system

There are Christian web-building programmes, such as www.Church123.com and www.churchinsight.com. The fees vary, but expect to pay a yearly charge. The advantages of an Internet-based web builder is that any authorised person can create as many pages as required and update content as often as needed; professional templates with appropriate graphics are provided; they can be customised easily to include pictures. Different people can be responsible for updating the pages – sharing the workload. If you can use a word processor then, with one of these systems, you can make an effective church site.

Learn how to do it yourself

Adult education colleges offer a range of website building courses, ranging from the basic (learning how to use Microsoft Front Page) to the advanced (Macromedia Studio). Note that website coding, graphic design and communication skills are quite different – you need all three to make a good site. Once someone knows how to create a site, it can be up and running quite quickly. However, the onus is on that individual to continue to update it, which could make it a chore rather than a pleasure. An adult education course will cost about £70 (rates vary around the country) and the software will add on another hefty chunk to the start-up costs (this varies according to the software you use). Results for DIY websites are variable, but a lot of the very worst church websites have been made this way. If you haven't made sites before then a church site should never be your test project.

Pay a professional to do it for you

The most expensive way is to find someone who creates websites for a living. They will charge professional rates, but hopefully give you a professional service in return. If you are a church that wants a totally bespoke cutting edge site then consider www.3sixtycreative.com. Obtain multiple quotes on larger projects as prices can vary.

For any of the above, weigh up the costs and the benefits. Don't be swayed by a huge list of features that you won't actually use. Likewise don't choose the cheapest option because it is the cheapest – look at what you get for your money, particularly support and advice. If applicable, ask the web designer to see examples of other sites that are already running and contact the churches for references.

Get the design right

People make snap judgments about websites: if yours doesn't come up to scratch visitors will leave quickly. Research published in a recent edition of the journal *Behaviour and Information Technology* revealed that decisions about a website are made in the blink of an eye. Canadian researchers from Carleton University in Ottawa tested this by showing a website for 50 milliseconds to volunteers. They then rated the sites according to their aesthetic appeal. The results were closely similar to their views on sites that they had spent longer visiting.

'Unless the first impression is favourable, visitors will be out of your site before they even know that you might be offering more than your competitors,' said Gitte Lindgaard, the project's lead researcher.

If this first impression – based on nothing more than the design choices, the colours and graphics – is positive then visitors will have a more favourable impression of the site's content.

Gordon Thorn, from *Church123*, agrees that this is the case. 'A bad website may stop people from ever visiting your church and may reinforce the stereotype that the church is out of touch and irrelevant,' he says.

So what makes a good design? It has to be simple and easy to read. Beyond that, the decision is yours, especially as the merits of a design often rely on opinion.

However, watch out for gimmicks – avoid background music, flashing text, rotating logos and moving picture slide shows. These are distractions, not attractions. Using them will detract from the most important things on the page: the words and will probably lead people away from the site not into it.

These graphics and other photos can also have large file sizes; each image on a website has to be loaded onto your computer before you can see them, how long it takes to download them depends on the visitor's Internet connection. While more than half the UK is connected to the Internet via broadband, you should design your site for those who don't.

Finally, ensure that the site is designed in such a way that it is easy to find your way around: the menu system (the list of site pages) should be visible either on the left hand side of the site or at the top. Don't try and reinvent the wheel and construct something crazy and new, we want people accessing the site and reading the Gospel, not tackling logic problems to get to the church's e-mail address.

Adding pictures to your site

A pure 'text only' site is visually very dull. A page with only fancy graphics suggests a lack of genuine content. A page full of mismatched clipart looks amateurish. But pages containing relevant pictures alongside the text will transform a website.

Choose the images carefully: if you want to illustrate what the church is like, you might think a picture of the building will suffice. Instead, take a picture of the people, for this truly shows what the church is like. Remember, people identify with people, not bricks. On your home page, you might consider having a headline that says 'People like you always welcome at Collinstone Community Church' with a picture of happy, smiling members of the church.

On the 'who's who' page, you can add in mugshots of the leadership team (for ideas on how to take these, see chapter 16). Pictures of the activities your church offers can be added ... the list is endless. All of these can be taken with a digital camera, or scanned in from photographs.

When uploading images to the site, remember that the picture needs to be 72dpi (dots per inch) or a low-resolution image, scaled to the right size and saved as an RGB image. This reduces the image to its optimum size for a computer screen and will download quickly, keeping your visitors happy.

The Internet also makes available a range of clipart and free picture sites specifically for the church, some of these are American in their focus, and might sit uncomfortably on a very traditional church website. Christian-run UK-based freefoto.com is a comprehensive database of different categories of pictures. These are free to use on-line for non-profit making websites, which includes your church. There are almost a million images to use and they can be easily adapted to offer images for harvest, summer days, Christmas etc.

Make the site accessible

Think of the partially-sighted people who will benefit from larger type sizes: pressing CTRL and the + key in most web browsers will increase the type size on most HTML formatted text. If your text is actually an image (say a JPEG graphic heading that says 'Church news') then this won't be enlarged or accessible to screen/Braille readers. Remember this when designing site graphics.

Make the text easy to read by choosing short column lengths, and don't justify the text as it's easier for the eye to read paragraphs set as left justified.

Be careful of the colours and graphics that you choose. If the site visitor is distracted by these then your design is a failure. The Royal National Institute for the Blind (RNIB) recommends choosing colours with a high level of contrast: for example, white text on a blue background. If the text is grey on a cyan background, it will be hard to read. A background graphic (such as a crest or shield) that has been tiled – so there's, say, six across the screen and 10 or so going down – can be very confusing, especially if you have text in a similar colour going across it at the same time. The RNIB recommend testing your site using a Colour Contrast Analyser, similar to the one offered by Vision Australia (www.visionaustralia.org.au) This free piece of software is an invaluable tool that will check the background and text colours to see if they are OK.

There is comprehensive advice on every aspect of website design for partially-sighted people available from the website www.rnib.org.uk. This covers everything from designing the site to making users aware of the accessibility options you've created. The RNIB also offers bespoke advice, for specific queries.

Register with search engines

Searching for something on the Internet has become second nature to many of us – we Google it. My honeymoon was the result of a Google search. Research in this book was Googled. If we want something from the Internet, we rely on the search engines (of which Google is the biggest) to help us.

A search engine works through keywords: hotels Jersey, church Collinstone etc. If the keywords that people will use to find your church appear throughout your site, and the site is registered with the search engine, then it will appear in the listings. It often takes a while for entries to appear on a search engine: anything from a few weeks to several months.

In addition to registering with all the main search engines, you should also sign up with www.findachurch.org.uk. This website offers a list of all the churches in every UK town, so people searching for a church will often end up here as it regularly appears high up search engine results. It's free to register the basic information on the site: the church's address, phone and fax numbers as well as an e-mail address. For a small yearly fee, the church is also listed with a photograph, an introduction and a link to your website. It might seem like another expense, but if it brings at least one person to the church each year then it's worth it.

Case study: Dagenham Baptist Church

A volunteer from Dagenham Baptist Church, Essex, set up a website for the church. For three years nothing happened to the site – no updates and spelling mistakes were left intact.

The church secretary, Jean Beavan, took over the task of working out how to update the site. First, she transferred the ownership of the domain name (www.dagenham baptists.org.uk) to the church, but couldn't update the site as she didn't have the appropriate software. Her inexperience with designing websites meant that while she was willing to try, she struggled, saying 'it all sounds quite complicated to me, like knitting on-line!'

The Dagenham site had been set up with one web hosting company who, on advising Mrs Beavan about her problems, told her to 'get someone else to build a website for you'. This wasn't what she wanted, so she approached a Christian web-building company. 'Can you assist one desperate novice please?' she asked.

The web builder software offered a free 30-day trial – and featured a range of templates and a free helpline, so the site was soon up and running.

The helpline reviewed her work and offered to make some improvements: the text colour was changed to make it more legible. A few appropriate graphics were added to liven up the pages, paragraphs were tweaked to make them more inviting and less relevant information was moved from the front page to the 'about us' page.

The site is clean and effective, includes the essential pages mentioned previously and each one is easily updatable. At the time of writing, the site has a home page offering a warm welcome; a visitors page outlining how their church works; a worship page highlighting the forthcoming services; a statement of belief; an Organisations page looks at the different groups that use the church; a page about Dagenham itself (useful for historians) and a page with directions and a diary of forthcoming events. On each page, the church's address and contact details are prominently displayed and because each page is clear and simple, it is fast to load and looks professional.

No doubt the site will have changed again by the time you read this, as Jean grows more confident in her web building skills.

Further reading

There is plenty of advice and information around on building great websites. Several monthly magazines are published and a quick Google search will bring up a wealth of possibilities. For specific advice on Christian websites, log on to www.hosea.co.uk.

THIRTEEN

NOT JUST FOR MAX CLIFFORD: NEWS STORIES AND PRESS RELEASES

The controversy over the 1979 film *The Life of Brian* is still remembered as yet another moment when people knew what the Church is against rather than for.

William Lyons, when writing about how churches worked with Disney to promote the first *Chronicles of Narnia* film in 2005, said, 'Monty Python's *Life of Brian* was appreciated by millions for its razor-edged satire on Christianity but was condemned by many clergymen as blasphemous. But the Narnia film ... has been seized on by churches as an opportunity to get a strong Christian message into popular culture.' (*Scotland on Sunday,* November 20, 2005).

So, here's a case of good news (the Church getting behind C.S. Lewis's ever-popular children's story) being tarnished by bad news from almost 30 years ago.

Here's Jeremy Clarkson, writing in *The Sun* (December 24, 2005): 'If I find myself sitting next to someone who's openly and militantly Christian, I usually get up from the table and run.' And what was he writing about? Some Christians who had been protesting outside the first partnership registration ceremonies (gay 'weddings') in Northern Ireland, just before Christmas 2005. In the season of peace and goodwill, the images of the Christian protestors brandishing placards that say 'Sodomy is sin' will stay in people's minds far more than a report in the *Daily Mirror* a few days later, about a church that was 'podcasting' its Sunday services. It will also stay in people's minds longer than their local parish priest's Christmas Eve sermon, or the nativity pictures or news of carol services that will have appeared in local papers in the run-up to the big day.

National newspapers have a duty to report what is going on in the world, and unfortunately, news isn't always good – and the old adage is that bad news sells papers whereas good news doesn't. After any disaster, sales of newspapers will rise as people want to find out what has happened.

However, many Christians miss the point: for the UK population to see that the Church is relevant and has a vital part to play in their lives today (and that Jesus is alive and wants to have a relationship with them) they need to find out how Christianity affects them in their small corner of the world. Churches need to make effective use of their local papers – in doing so, letting the local neighbourhood know what their community's fellowships are for, not what they are against.

Some Christians will feel uncomfortable with boasting about the work that they do. In Galatians 6:14, Paul writes, 'May I never boast except in the cross of our Lord Jesus Christ, through which the world has been crucified to me, and I to the world.' Boasting about the achievements of our churches might seem to be unchristian but to put this in perspective:

without boasting, you won't be witnessing. A good story in your local newspaper will speak volumes about both the Gospel and the local church.

But what makes a good news story for your local paper? The key to sending in information (press releases) is to determine what your local media outlets are looking for. News can be broken down into categories: it can be a new event that has happened, it can be new information based on that event or it could be something new that has been said, produced, found or discovered, especially by someone in a public position. So, by this definition, the Archbishop of Canterbury resigning is a national news story, but the stepping down of a church deacon isn't. Likewise, if your church deacon happens to think that global warming is caused by the length of your pastor's sermons, that's not national news. But if the Archbishop of Canterbury has said we need shorter sermons to prevent global warming then it would hit the headlines. Why should his opinion count more than your deacon? Because his judgments affect more people.

News is often bad – news that if it happened to you, you'd rather people didn't know about it. The most common example is politicians who suddenly find their private lives splashed all over the newspapers, such as the infamous 'MP David Mellor in a Chelsea football outfit' incident. Every so often a church-related bad news story breaks, such as a child-abuse scandal or a dispute between a minister and the organist that has escalated into a real 'Neighbours From Hell' situation. In nearly all cases, these tend to focus on Church of England or Catholic churches as they are seen as the 'established' churches in the UK. While the publicity is often unwelcome, it is much easier to have everything in the open as it lances the boil of public curiosity.

News can also be unusual or unpredictable events – which is why, come the time of major charity fundraising events, you'll find newspapers devoting space to people willing to sit in a bathtub of beans raising hundreds of pounds in the process, rather than those individuals who quietly and without ceremony slipped a couple of thousand pounds into the collection plate. The difference is not in the amount raised, but in how it was raised – the how becomes the news story.

Another aspect to news is how things affect the way we live: it could be the cost of housing, petrol, how much people give to church, church attendance figures, school or hospital league tables, the price of a pint. This is about how the money we earn can be spent, and often the news is given personal touches. You'll see this every year after the Budget: to try and make the financial figures understandable, journalists will tell you how the average family groups will be affected, before offering you a personal calculator. This focus on people is another press fixation, especially local journalism: how does this news affect a group of people?

When Kelvin MacKenzie was the editor of *The Sun*, he wanted every page to have that 'gee whizz, Doris!' factor. He did this with his own maxim – shock and amaze on every page. He wanted people to talk about the paper. So, news can often be amazing, astounding and surprising. Often it records, such as the slowest person to complete the London Marathon, sometimes it's unusual libel payouts in the courts, and sometimes – well, it's just something that makes you smile, such as cute animal pictures.

Another way of looking at a newspaper is the original slogan for *The News of the World*: all human life is here. Newspapers don't discriminate, news is news, regardless of who it happens to. Of course, themed newspapers will serve different markets, so you'd not expect to find Muslim news in the *Methodist Recorder* – but they will want to cover news from a Methodist perspective, or find the 'Methodist angle'. So, for example, should there be an earthquake, the paper will naturally find out if there are any Methodist casualties and how Methodists are helping with the clear-up operations. Sometimes this can make a minority interest newspaper appear parochial; at the same time, it shows the target audience how they have been affected or caught up within that event.

News happens, and with the Internet there is more news out there than there ever has been before. Newspapers are fatter than they were 20 years ago, there are more radio stations offering more news bulletins, and the rise in the number of television stations means that there is also a rash of 24-hour rolling news channels. There will always be a demand for new news. God created us to be curious creatures and that will always be the case. Please don't think that your church news doesn't matter, or isn't of interest to your local newspapers and radio stations. Forget trying to tell the nationals that your church has raised £127.57 at a bring and buy sale: what happens in Collinstone is of no relevance to the readers in Derby. But, this is of interest to your local paper.

When I encourage local churches to send news items into their local paper, the common complaint is that 'we tried before and they didn't print it.' Why should that be a reason to give up? It's a defeatist attitude. You are not under siege and the local newspaper does not have an agenda against your church.

Indeed, many local newspapers would actually appreciate knowing where their local church is. One of my former editors confided that in all the time he had been producing that paper the local parish priests had not once popped their head round the door to introduce themselves – an attitude he found odd, equally so when the paper received regular calls from the local mosques and Sikh temples giving updates on what good works they had been doing lately.

The next problem that journalists face is arrogance: sometimes people expect the news that their church has raised £10.51 during a sponsored hop to appear on the front page. When the story then doesn't appear, or isn't in the anticipated form, the disgruntled party demands an explanation from whoever picks up the phone, regardless of whether they know anything about the story or not – this aggravates the caller even more. More often than not, it hasn't been included due to a lack of space, or there are other reasons. A story goes from a reporter to a news editor to a sub-editor. The sub has to ensure that all the words fit the space available – which often changes. Both the news editor and the sub-editor will make subjective judgments about a story without being over-protective about unnecessary details. This editing often changes the structure of the story: sub-editors usually cut text from the bottom of the story, so journalists write to ensure all the facts appear at the top. The page is then sent to the editor to approve. This means that every story is seen by at least four people, and no one is out to make a deliberate mistake.

If your story doesn't appear in print or it doesn't appear at the length you'd expected, don't assume it had a right to be, or it was left out maliciously – be gracious, and don't let it put you off sending in other stories: not every press release I send gets printed!

Press releases are a form of creative writing, in that someone has worked hard to create it. Naturally, people become protective of their release and end up demanding that it's either printed word for word or that they see the version of the report before it goes to press. If you make similar demands you're setting yourself up for a massive fall. Here's an example that a church demanded was printed as submitted (names and the event have been changed to protect the church).

> 'If you where looking for this first ever Collinstone Family Carnival to of been a damp squid – no hope event after the morning heavy rain then you can forget it. The People of Collinstone proofed that this Community wants to have fun come rain or sunshine, they sent out a clear call to all the organizing committee, volunteers, local business fraternity and sponsors that this event is here to stay by turning out in greater numbers than anyone would of perceived.'

This is just the first paragraph of a very long release that just waffles – and it wasn't proofread before being sent. While you can just about work out what happened, who on earth predicted that the event would be a 'damp squid' rather than a 'damp squib'? This subtle difference would damage the reputation of the newspaper rather than the church, had the release been printed in full. We'll come back to this release later, as it will form the template for sending out a press release to local newspapers.

What information are journalists actually after? Every newspaper or radio station has different criteria; read or listen to find out. This is the information that *The Baptist Times* offers to its readers:

1. Send it in as soon as you can.
2. Tell us WHAT the event was, WHEN it happened, WHERE it was, WHO was involved and WHY it was important.
3. Assume we don't know anything except what you tell us. If you mention a person we need to know who they are. Don't use acronyms without explaining them.

4. Try and include quotes – what did it actually mean to people?
5. Always try to include a contact number for people who are available during the day.
6. A good picture often makes the story.
7. If the picture is of a person, we need to know who it is.
8. Who took the picture?

It's simple and straightforward. Over the next few pages we'll break it down and use this information to rework the press release.

Send it in as soon as you can

Newspapers usually assign reporters a district to cover and some also have a religious affairs correspondent. Sending in press releases or talking to your local reporter is more effective than a scattergun approach of just sending a release to the newsdesk. You should also find out when the paper goes to press (off-stone is the technical term) – there is no point in calling up your local newspaper at 4 p.m. on a Wednesday to let them know that you're holding a jumble sale on Saturday when the paper comes out on Thursday morning. You're asking for the journalists to do a stop press, something that will rarely happen.

Sending information over far too late is the most common problem for many churches trying to get their news into the paper. There are two ways of looking at this: an event that is about to happen and an event which has just happened. Remember there is nothing as old as yesterday's news. Don't wait! Plan ahead and ensure that you get the information over at the appropriate time. If the event took place on Sunday morning, such as a baptismal service, send the release no later than Monday morning. If the event took place on a Wednesday evening – your women's group could have had a special guest speaker – ensure that the relevant information is sent by Thursday lunchtime. Time is of the essence, and the more notice you give your journalist then the more likely it will be that the story will be used.

Likewise, don't wait for the photos to come back before submitting them. With most people now knowing someone who owns a digital camera, there should be no excuse for sending in prints: send a digital file via your computer. If you only have a 35mm camera, then take the film in to be developed on the fastest service available. This won't be reimbursed by the newspaper, but if you've taken a decent photo it will be worth the processing charge. This cost might be claimable from your church's publicity budget. How to take and send pictures to newspapers will be covered in detail in chapter 16.

That's all very well for events that have just happened, but what about the events that are about to happen? Give journalists at least three weeks' notice of the cover date nearest to the event. A cover date is the date of that issue – if your event takes place on Saturday 20th, and your paper is published on Thursdays, then the edition you need to work towards is Thursday 18th. Working backwards, three weeks from that Thursday is the 4th. So ensure that you have all the advance information sent over to the journalists by that day – aim for a few days before and you'll give yourself breathing space if you're a few days late.

Why should you send information over so early? It's about forward planning. If the information is sent over early enough then you can have some 'forthcoming attraction' type notices: 'Collinstone Community Church is holding a boot fair on

Saturday 20th, to book your pitch call 567890', for example. That will help generate awareness of the event and encourage people to go along. The second reason is it gives the journalist a chance to discern whether the event is photogenic enough to send along one of the paper's photographers. Most local newspapers employ a team of hardworking photographers who have limited time to take the pictures that everyone wants. They will be on a tight timescale and can only pop in to take the pictures, some information about who is in them and then go again. It's unreasonable to expect the photographer to stay and snap away for the whole event – plan ahead, you can help the journalist coordinating the story: in the release, say (for example) 'Photo opportunity: at 2.45 p.m., the new buildings will be opened by the mayor, the minister and the bishop.' In doing so, you create a definite moment for the photographers' diary, rather than letting them turn up and wait for you to assemble the appropriate people or hope that they will be able to do their best.

You will also need to think about the practicalities of a photocall. If there are parts of the building that hold particular holy significance, or a flash bulb could damage an old painting, then ensure that the photographer knows that this area is off-limits. Let the photographer know if there's a balcony that can be climbed up to take pictures from, as height can create interesting angles. Also think about who is going to be photographed: if there are people who would rather not have their pictures in the paper, then warn them in advance and let them sit in a certain part of the building. If the photographer is coming to take pictures of some children's work, then let the parents know beforehand. While most parents will be happy for their children to appear in the paper, some will not give their consent. The photographer will not know which child falls into which category, so the onus is on you to ensure that the children are appropriately separated to avoid embarrassment.

You can also help the photographer by giving them a list of who's who, with correct spellings of the names and their job titles.

The What, When, Where, Who and Why?

Every news story can be brought back to these small words: if they don't tell the what, the when, the where, the who and the why then it's not a news story, it's a report for insiders. Make sure you answer these basic questions when writing a press release:

What is it that you are writing a press release about?

One of my former editors, when asking us what a story was about, would ask: 'What is the top-line?' Or, in non-journalese, 'In one sentence, sum up the story'. It might be 'Church raises £159.54 in sponsored silence', 'teenager needs to raise £10,000 to help disadvantaged children in Senegal' or 'new pastor for Collinstone'. What it won't be is something long-winded, such as 'It was a great day at Collinstone when, in sunny warm weather, the church members, deacons and bishop welcomed the arrival of the Revd Roger Boucher at his induction service on Saturday afternoon, followed by a splendid slap-up feast arranged by church members Sid and Doris Faithful'. This is a real mouthful and you're lost completely by the time you get to the first mention of the church members. Stick to the facts, don't embellish too much: 'Collinstone Community Church welcomed the Revd Roger Boucher as its new pastor at a special service on Saturday' or 'The Revd Roger Boucher was inducted as the new pastor of Collinstone Community Church on Saturday' is all that needs to be said.

When did all this happen? Or when will it happen?

Be accurate with your dates and times (don't suggest that morning worship takes place at 11 p.m.). If you send a release to the papers about the induction of Roger Boucher on Thursday 1st and say it takes place on Saturday, then is that Saturday 3rd or Saturday 10th? If the induction took place on Saturday 3rd and the release is sent on Monday 12th, then be clear that the release states the service was on Saturday 3rd, and not Saturday 10th – but don't leave it that long to send it in, it's old news by then!

Where did it happen?

This might seem obvious: the induction took place at the church. But was it in the church hall or the sanctuary? Perhaps you had to hire the leisure centre as you needed the extra space. It's also important to check the spellings: if refreshments were served in the large hall, which is formally known as the Allan Richie Hall, then make sure that you use that detail, and ensure that you check whether it's Allen or Allan.

Who is involved in the story?

For some press releases, it's obvious. The teenager who wants to raise £10,000 to go on a summer mission to Senegal is the focus of that release. A pastor's induction will be focused on them, and the people who were leading and speaking at the service. If local dignitaries were present, you should also list their attendance (unless they attend in a personal capacity and not representing their office). If the church is planning a rebuilding scheme, you might include quotes from the church leaders, the chair of the rebuilding team, any councillors involved in helping gain planning permission and local residents who will use the expanded church buildings. Don't include quotes from 'one attendee' or 'a bystander', along the lines of: '"It was a tremendous day," said one attendee.' These people are nameless and as useful to us as 'a source revealed' or 'a TV insider' which populate national newspapers like the plague. It's quite obvious that these quotes can be made up, as there is no real person to attribute the words to.

Why is this event important? Or why are you sending the release in?

This is the real check and balance to your release – what is the reason that this release has been created? Adam Spurgeon wants people to read the story in the paper and send donations to help him reach his £10,000 target; but he also wants to make the world a better place. The induction of Roger Boucher as Collinstone's pastor is news because the church wants to let the local community know that they have a new minister ready to help with any pastoral needs. The sponsored silence is news because the church has gained another £160 for its steeple restoration fund. Just sending in a release saying that your church meets for worship at 10.30 a.m. every Sunday is not news: it's the same information that has been available for years. If the church is moving its service times to 10.45 a.m. to accommodate an extra morning service at 9 a.m., then that's news.

*Assume the only details they know are what you tell
them. If you mention a person, who are they? Don't use
acronyms without explaining them*

When I was a young schoolboy, we had to write news reports
of what we did at the weekend – that weekend, my parents had
taken me to visit their friends from church, the Taits. As a five-
year-old, I had no idea how to spell their name, but my teacher
would know – she knows everything. It was a good lesson to
learn: my teacher didn't know the clan Tait and therefore could
only offer 'Tate'. Likewise, when I read a book with the baffling
acronyms R/T and MP, my dad was able to help: radio telephone
and Member of Parliament. Had he not been around, I'd have
been none the wiser. Picture the bemusement on the face of a
journalist trying to work out what the acronym CHIPS could
stand for – Collinstone Historical Information Picture Society
perhaps? Don't leave it to chance, spell out the acronym.

Who are the people that you mention? You might know
that Mary Jones is your church's pastor, but the reader of the
newspaper won't unless you tell them. One way that you can
iron this out is to ask a non-churchgoing friend to proofread
any release before submission.

It's also worth remembering the correct usage of the title
'the Revd'. Most newspapers will call a minister or pastor 'the
Rev' all the way through the text: 'Rev Jones said'. The correct
way is 'the Revd Andrew Jones' for the first mention and then
Mr Jones thereafter. Some ministers and pastors don't like
being singled out with this title; if this is the case then, in
the notes to the editor at the end of the release, you can state
something like this: 'although Andrew Jones is an ordained
minister, please do not call him "the Rev", he is pastor/team
leader of the church.'

Include quotes – what did it actually mean to people?

Facts are all very well, but they can be terribly boring. How many people have read the dictionary or the *Guinness Book of Records* as if they were novels? And how often have you read the lists in the Bible – can you tell me who begat whom? A news story is always more interesting if you can get a quote attached to it: sometimes in national newspapers this is the infamous 'insider', but for your church press releases it is often the organiser, or the pastor. Quotes are a way of putting emotion into a story: how did it affect you? What did it mean to you? Compare 'The church was full' with 'It was brilliant – the church was packed to the rafters and we could really feel God's presence with us.' Which one shows more emotion?

You should also attempt to make your quotes mention Jesus – it makes it harder for him to be edited out by the journalist later, and we shouldn't be ashamed of the reason why we do things as a church.

Collinstone Community Church has opened an extension paid for solely by church members' donations. Here are some possible quotes that you could put in a press release: 'We know Jesus loves Collinstone and we want to show some of that love by opening this facility up for their use.'

'We don't have any millionaires in our church, this was achieved by a bunch of ordinary people who put God first in their lives.'

Always include a contact number for people who are available during the day

What's the point in sending in a press release and not giving the journalist an opportunity to ask any follow-up questions? Most journalists on local papers try and work normal office hours, and will want to find out more information during these hours. It's worth offering two numbers – for different people – to make it easier for a journalist to contact one of the organisers. If you're a minister and have a mobile phone which is used for family and close friends only, think carefully before giving that number to the press: will you mind journalists contacting you on your day off to ask for a quote? Or would you prefer to ensure all your business is carried out through your church office? There is no right answer; it depends on what you'd prefer.

A good picture often makes the story

'A picture paints a thousand words' is a cliché because it's true. I could describe the clothes I'm wearing to you in detail – the colours, the styles, the flares. I could also convince you that I was actually Adonis, rather than the flabby out-of-shape beer monster that is the reality. But, it's much easier to show you a picture: you can visualise something easily if you have reference points to turn to. So, when planning a press release think carefully about whether you can offer a picture to accompany it. This might be of the event (for a press release sent afterwards), of a similar event (a previous boot sale, say) or even just head and shoulders pictures (mugshots) of the church's pastor. Never send them as part of a word processing file or an ink-jet print out – always send them as hi-res jpeg files or actual photographs. Chapter 16 will explain this in more detail.

Who's who?

If you're sending a picture of Mary Jones, the church's pastor, and including a quote from her and Ann Letts, the church's Woman's Own leader, then make sure any picture has a caption: 'picture is of Mary Jones, pastor of Collinstone Community Church.' If it's a group shot, then the press release must state the order in which people appear, such as: 'Launching the event are (from left) Mary Jones, pastor of the church and Ann Letts, leader of the Woman's Own group'. Don't leave it to chance.

Who took the picture?

Some newspapers like to give the photographer credit – not all will, but it's always worth ensuring that this information is available.

Putting this into practice: a sample press release

Taking all this information, we can then turn back to the press release for the Collinstone Community Carnival. We want to create a press release that we can send to the Collinstone Chronicle.

PRESS RELEASE – Monday, August 15

Rain doesn't deter party spirit

The first Collinstone Community Church carnival attracted a large crowd of revellers, despite heavy rain. The event, which took place on Saturday afternoon, had been threatened with downpours in the morning, but people still came out to enjoy a range of activities including live music and dancing and a range of traditional fairground rides.

The carnival was held at the recreation ground and featured several marquees

Activities included karaoke, free face painting, balloons and prizes. A range of stalls offering games and bric-a-brac were offered and carnival goers could also enjoy a barbecue.

The mayor opened the carnival, and gave a speech. 'I'm honoured to open the first Collinstone Community Carnival,' she said.

The mayor also presented prizes to Brianna Cain (13) and Lucy Walsh (11), winner and runner-up of the competition to design a poster to publicise the carnival.

Lloyd Hinton, a local artist studying at Collinstone University, made some sketches of the day. These will go on display in the Community Church at a later date.

The event was organised by Collinstone Community Church, and sponsored by local businesses. Monies raised from the event – currently £1234 – will go towards the town's regeneration project.

Gary Dicks, chairman of the carnival committee said, 'We're grateful to God that the weather held and that the carnival was a massive success. We wanted to show the community that following Jesus doesn't mean you can't have fun – we were delighted with the turnout, it seems that the town really wants to enjoy themselves. This will become an annual event.'

* ENDS *

Notes to editors:

- A picture of Lucy Higgins (9) coming down the helter-skelter is attached. It was taken by Paul Walters.
- For more information, please contact Gary Dicks, the chairman, on (01234) 567890 or Mary Jones, Collinstone Community Church's pastor on (01234) 098765.
- The carnival was held to raise funds for the town's regeneration project. So far, the church has raised £1234.

- The carnival is one of a number of community events organised by the church. Other initiatives include a litter collection, a quiz night and an Alpha course.
- The church holds services on Sundays at 10 a.m. and 6.30 p.m.

Sending in your church newsletter

Don't send in anything to a newspaper that you wouldn't want to see in print. If you send in your monthly newsletter, be certain that the information it contains is suitable for a wider circulation. Obviously, if your newsletter is distributed to non-churchgoers then this isn't as much of a problem. If you send a newsletter into a newspaper, they will make the assumption that it is okay to take information from it to use for their stories.

It's always worth sending in your church newsletter, not just to the local paper but also to your denominational newspapers, such as *The Church of England Newspaper* or *The Baptist Times*. If you do have sensitive information, such as details of a missionary's work in a sensitive location, then staple a short note to the front of the newsletter stating that this item is not for publication. Unless it is stapled, you run the risk of your request going astray. Likewise, if you have any particular event you wish to highlight then you should also staple a note to the front of the news-sheet – 'This issue features an article by Andy Lingard who has just returned from 10 months working with Aids orphans in Malawi.'

Sharing your good news in your local newspapers is brilliant: it can act as a morale booster for the fellowship and help enhance the church's reputation in its neighbourhood. Hopefully, in so doing, it will attract people to Christ in the process.

FOURTEEN

DAMAGE LIMITATION AND GOOD PUBLICITY: NEWSPAPER INTERVIEWS

I t's one thing sending in press releases to newspapers, but what about when a newspaper contacts you asking for a comment? There will be occasions when a church is at the centre of a news story: a member of the congregation is killed unexpectedly; someone is attacked on the premises; the worshippers are too noisy; or there is an allegation of child abuse or adultery. These are some of the circumstances that might cause a newspaper to get in touch with you. Knowing how to respond, especially if you are a volunteer there, is difficult, as there is no right or wrong way.

If you have to deal with bad news and you know that it is forthcoming, the church leadership team should contact the communications department of either the denomination's national headquarters or the regional offices. It might be possible for them to prepare a press statement and request that all correspondence be directed to them. This should give you an extra buffer zone, and help cope with numerous reporters calling you in the search for a new angle on the story.

However, never refuse to talk to the press. Here are some reasons why. If the church is invited to comment on a council's plans to build seven skyscrapers in the church's car park without asking first, the reporter might ask, 'Would you agree the new housing policy has some flaws?' The church pastor might agree that this is unreasonable, but not be sure what to say, so end up giving a monosyllabic answer: 'Yes'. No further comment and the headline might end up as thus:

MINISTER SLAMS COUNCIL

You might find that it's your church where members have been accused of parking on the pavement and blocking access for pedestrians. Rather than admitting that there is a problem, it is tempting to try and deny it – the 'sweep it under the carpet' approach only makes things worse in the long run. The reporter will ask a question like this: 'Are you encouraging your congregation to park on the pavements?' The minister, in full denial mode, replies with a 'No'. The headline that then appears is:

MINISTER DENIES BLOCKING PAVEMENTS

When dealing with bad news it is hard to know exactly how to respond to the allegations. It might be tempting to refuse to talk to a journalist, offering a 'no comment' instead. This too is a mistake, as it could lead to a headline such as this:

DRUGS BUST: MINISTER REFUSES COMMENT

If you are involved in this kind of situation, then choose your words carefully. Don't be afraid to ask the journalist to give you five minutes to collect your thoughts (or even prepare a written statement to give them); ask them what questions they'd like answered, get their direct line and think and pray about your answers. Then call them back. You won't be saying something in the heat of the moment – instead you'll have a chance to say what needs to be said.

Journalists shouldn't contact you for a quote if a case like one of those above has become a criminal prosecution: in order to ensure a fair trial, the law forbids any expanding of a news story as soon as someone is charged for a crime or a warrant for their arrest is made. Likewise, avoid referring to such cases in your church newsletter.

If you are asked to comment on the tragic death of someone in your fellowship, especially in the wake of a disaster such as a train crash, don't assume that the newspaper's readers have a right to know about the life of the person killed. Some basic details always help flesh out news reports – the name, age, profession, family and so on are always helpful, but it could be said that 'he/she was a very private person.' When asked for a comment in cases like this, you could always start your quote with something like this: 'I credit your readers with enough compassion to allow this family to grieve in peace.' However, they might ask the minister to speak on their behalf. In such a case, it would be worth preparing a short statement and eulogy to release to the press. Your denomination's press office should be able to give you assistance should it be needed.

Similarly, should there be a tragic event on your church premises, such as a mugging, then choose your words with care. Regardless of what the church could have done to prevent the attack, or not, do not ascribe blame to the person who has been attacked: never say, 'We had adequate lighting and CCTV, so it was her fault for walking down there late at night.' Show

Christian love and compassion! 'Before I answer that, let me say on behalf of the whole fellowship that our thoughts and prayers are with Mrs Smith, and I'll be seeing her in hospital later today …' Think of the implication that such a statement means: instead of searching for blame and a criminal, the church is doing what it should be doing: showing practical love and care. Anyone reading that quote can't miss the Christian take on what has happened, and instead of thinking that the church or minister is busy playing a blame game, they are actually concentrating their thoughts very much on the victim.

All these hard-hitting headlines are rare: most of the time reporters – particularly local ones who will have to approach you again in the future – are by and large trying to get to the facts and not to stitch the Church up.

Finally, and this will be difficult especially if you are dealing with an emotional event, try and be helpful to the journalist: be objective and remember that most journalists are simply trying to report the facts, not mount a personal attack on the church or Christianity. One of the reasons for this is that you have a unique opportunity to witness to the reporter: your conduct is that witnessing tool. What would Jesus do in these situations? That's not for me to say, but if we want the journalist to know that we have a living faith in a God who loved them enough to send Jesus, our behaviour must be Christ-like.

The reporter is also a human being. They have bills to pay, cats to feed, children to look after and deadlines to meet. While they are using you for the purposes of their story, they are also worrying about the same day-to-day issues that you will be fretting about. You can always ask them questions: Have you been on the paper long? Do you live locally? Do you have a family? What time will you get home tonight? If appropriate, ask if there is anything that you could pray for them in your own time – these are things that help build up a relationship between you and the journalist.

This is especially important if you are talking to your district reporter who has to find bits to fill their neighbourhood news column: if you make yourself approachable and can also offer useable news stories then they will frequently call you asking if you have any news. You become a contact for them, and they will value you for that. In turn, the church gets its name in the paper frequently, and the public image of your church will not be one of a sleepy little fellowship where nice people turn up and go home again, but a bustling church where the Gospel means social action that makes the world a better place.

FIFTEEN

GOING LIVE:
APPEARING ON RADIO
OR TELEVISION

Many BBC local radio stations have a Sunday morning 'God-slot', and community radio stations do local news featuring local people. They will always be on the look-out for interesting stories. Sending them your church newsletter and press releases is always worthwhile, but there's no need to include pictures for the radio! Listen to your local BBC Sunday show, usually broadcast between 6 a.m. and 9 a.m., to find out what type of programme it is, as they vary.

Over the past few years, I've been interviewed by different radio stations. Some I've done from my bed, others have meant getting up early and visiting studios. It's always worthwhile and your words have an opportunity to speak to people at home, especially for those who rely on this as part of their Sunday worship. These have nearly always been live broadcasts, but interviews are sometimes recorded to be inserted into the show.

An interview is rarely done 'cold': before the slot, the interviewer discusses the direction they want it to take, the questions that will come up and the approximate length. This gives some time to prepare yourself. Before going to the studio, on one side of a sheet make some notes about your subject: facts and figures, notable quotes and perhaps even a sound bite. Clearly lay these out in large letters so that they are easily accessible. If it is a closely typed manuscript, then you won't 'think on your feet' so well, you'll spend most of the interview looking for the right part of the page. And the best interviewees barely look at their notes – use them for emergencies!

Don't memorise your phrases as you'll come across as robotic rather than natural. The reporter will tell you whether it's a long interview or a short quote for a news story. If it's the latter, don't waffle; think about how you can get your point across as succinctly as possible and still be interesting.

You will be sat in the right position for the microphone to pick up your voice. I forgot this on my first interview with Premier Christian Radio: sat too far away from the microphone and speaking hesitantly, I sounded very feeble and lacking authority. A good lesson learnt.

Watch the 'ums' and 'errs' – it doesn't make good radio. If you're unsure how you'll do, practise with a friend: give them something like a squeaky toy, get them to ask you questions and if you um or err, let them squeak! You'll be able to train yourself not to be so hesitant.

There is no need to answer questions immediately, especially if you're nervous. Pause for a second to collect your thoughts and then speak. If you just gabble away with the first thing that comes into your head, you will probably speak too fast and lose track of your thoughts halfway through the sentence (this is where notes prove to be invaluable).

Keep an eye on the interviewer as they will often encourage you to keep talking or to bring your reply to a close so they can ask the next question. It's worth remembering that a smile can be heard when your face can't be seen: even though people can't see you they will still form a first impression of you within the first 30 seconds of your appearance. Try to sound cheerful, knowledgeable and open, rather than angry, arrogant or closed.

Panel interviews

If you're taking part in a panel discussion, then before appearing, do some homework: not just on the subject but on who is on the panel. There's nothing worse than turning up and not realising that you're taking part in a one-sided debate on a hot issue. This isn't a case of you turning into a detective and looking to dish some dirt on your opponent's private life and using the Church as an excuse to give you the moral high ground. No, find out what field the other panel members are experts in: you would not debate with Professor Richard Dawkins without knowing his academic qualifications and his views on religion. If you were appearing with someone from the British Humanist Society, it would be wise to know that the number of people who belong to the organisation is estimated to be around five thousand – while seven million people go to church every week. It's a great fact, which should help make your point about the Church's continued relevance to our world.

Find out if the interview will be recorded in advance or whether it will be live: if recorded you might have an opportunity to restart your answers if you fluff them.

It's also worth watching *Question Time* or *Newsnight* to see how politicians cope with answering questions under pressure. Sometimes, they might not answer the question in the way you expect. This is particularly useful if you have a point you wish to make, but you're not sure how to make it. Instead of answering 'yes, but ...' you could just say 'I think the real question is ...' and away you go.

Dressing for television

If you're appearing on a television interview, then be yourself and dress appropriately to your usual job or position. If you usually wear an open-neck shirt rather than a dog collar or a tie, then stick to that. People will look at you when you're on telly – if you're wearing distracting clothes then the viewer will stop listening and start thinking 'What an ugly tie' or 'What a weirdly coloured T-shirt.' Therefore, it's always worth looking smart and slightly fashionable. Many Christians don't follow fashion, so appearing on television in a comfy old gardening jumper or a suit that was fashionable in the 1950s, reinforces the view that Christians are from another planet.

Check with your contact at the television station that wearing a blue or green tie won't interfere with the show; some programmes are produced from a computer-generated studio where the newscaster sits in an all-green or all-blue studio and the graphics and set are added in electronically. If you wear a colour that is the same shade as the background then you run the risk of becoming a floating head rather than a talking head.

Don't be afraid

Don't be afraid of taking part in radio or television debates, especially if you are a church leader. However, pray before you appear, particularly that the Holy Spirit will give you the right words to say. Relish the challenge and remember that the way you come across, as well as the words that come out of your mouth, will reflect on the Church as a whole.

SIXTEEN

SMILE PLEASE, YOU'RE ON CAMERA! TAKING PICTURES

There are three ways in which pictures end up being used in newspapers. If the paper has a photographer, they might be sent along to the event to take their own pictures. The second way is for you to employ a freelance photographer. You will get great results, but at a price. So you might prefer to take your own. The advantage of this is that you can be on hand for the whole event and can take more photos, especially with a digital camera.

Pictures can tell a news story far better than a press release can by itself. But, a lifeless picture, poorly taken and with no spark of imagination will paint a bleak portrait of your fellowship, particularly as you'll instantly be conforming to the stereotype of boring Christians doing boring things that are irrelevant to the modern world.

The trouble is that so many pictures taken by churches for use in local media are unsuitable for reproduction. It's not just the way the photograph is composed that can cause problems, but also the way it is submitted. In this chapter, we'll take apart a bad photo and put it back together again. A typical church photograph will be of an event that has taken place – a building opening, a fun day or a new minister. There is plenty of scope for an interesting picture in each case, so why do people choose to send in a line of people, all neatly standing in a row as if waiting for the firing squad? Men in grey suits do not make exciting images.

Think carefully about how to take your photographs. Now that digital cameras have taken over, our pictures have changed forever. There is no need to stand patiently watching the birdie – as long as there's enough battery power, you can take as many pictures as you need. Regardless of whether you're using 35mm film or a digital camera, the biggest mistake that people make when taking any photograph is that they take it only once. The fewer photographs you take, the greater the odds you have of having a bad photograph.

For our wedding photos, my wife and I wanted a picture of everyone who attended. The first shot was out of focus, the second, thanks to a malfunctioning flash, was too dark. The third one was in focus, the lighting was right but people weren't smiling. Thankfully, the fourth one was perfect and our wedding photo was saved. You might not be taking a crowd shot of 150 plus people, but the same principle applies. If you take just a couple of photos, you run the risk of taking duff ones. With large digital memory cards, you can take a good selection of pictures and then select the best ones.

Get the resolution right

Digital cameras usually allow you to choose the resolution for the picture; the smaller the image size, the more photos you can save. If a newspaper is going to use your pictures, it will want the largest possible. Professionals talk in dots per inch. The more dots there are to an inch, the better the image will be. Save your image in large resolution. While it creates a larger file, it is a resolution that is large enough for even a magazine to cope with.

Don't send ink jet prints

It's very tempting to help your newspaper by printing out the image onto the special photo paper recommended by your printer manufacturer. You might think that you're doing them a favour, as all they'll have to do is scan it and it's ready to make the news. This small favour causes work, so your efforts might be overlooked in favour of a digital image when deadline looms. An inkjet print is made up of thousands of tiny dots – get a magnifying glass out and have a look. When it's scanned, all those tiny dots are replicated by the scanner. Because the surface of the paper you printed to is uneven, the computer scans all the flaws, and the new image is poorer. Thanks to the miracles of photo-editing software, it's possible to cover for some of these defects, but not all. It's much better to email press releases containing a photo to the newspaper – if they choose to use the picture, they can forward it straight onto the picture desk.

Filenames

The filename that you choose to give to the file is equally important. Digital cameras give sequential codes, IMG_ 2876.jpg is one from mine. This means nothing to me, let alone the picture desk of your local newspaper. In this case,

The difference between an ink jet print-out and a digital image is dramatic

the picture is of some prize-winning dogs, the file could have been renamed 'StLukes_dogshow.jpg', ensuring that the name was directly relevant to the press release sent in.

Submitting physical prints

If you submit a picture from a 35mm camera, don't feel that you're still in the dark ages. Newspapers still work from this type of photo, and they'll produce great results. Glossy paper is easier to scan than matt, but if possible, submit the photo and the negative strip. You should stipulate that the negative strip and/or photograph must be returned. Most newspapers use negative scanners, giving the highest quality scans.

Find out what they want

Are you unsure about what your local newspaper will want? Give them a call. At certain times, the newspaper office will be busier than others, especially when they have to get the paper off-stone. If you've picked the wrong moment to speak to the photographic desk then don't be offended if they are to the point: you could be holding up the press. Think about what you want to ask, concisely explain who you are, what you want to do and ask them how they want the pictures submitted. If you don't understand anything, say so. And if you try and help the newspaper by giving them what they want, it's more likely they can use your pictures.

They will also tell you how to submit pictures to them. If this is a digital picture by email and you have no experience of doing this, they should be able to help you.

Shooting children

Are you hosting a children's event and want to take pictures of it, but you need to protect the children's identity? Well, it's not illegal to take a photo of children having fun. And happy children happen to be very photogenic, often making front page news of a local paper if the picture is good enough. Yet many people are scared of taking children's pictures in case they are misused by others. This is quite restrictive. Yet, newspaper editors work in accordance with the Press Complaints Commission's Code of Practice. This commonsense set of guidelines actually gives a newspaper clear advice on how and when to take pictures of children. This is what it says:

'A child under 16 must not be interviewed or photographed on issues involving their own or another child's welfare unless a custodial parent or similarly responsible adult consents.

'Pupils must not be approached or photographed at school without the permission of the school authorities.'

So, if you're holding a holiday Bible club and want to invite a photographer from your local newspaper, or take pictures yourself, all you need to do is ask the parents for their permission. Do this when registering them on the first day: add a line on the consent form that says, 'I do/do not give my consent for photos to be taken of my child that can be used in publicising the holiday club'.

Get the right angle

If you snap away you can experiment with the angle it is taken from. The majority of bad pictures are taken with the photographer standing upright, with the camera stuck to the face. What if the photographer took the picture while standing

on a chair looking down? Or from the pulpit? Alternatively, the photographer might kneel down and point the camera upwards. A little experimentation gives great results.

Turning a bad photograph into a masterpiece

This is an example based on a real event. Collinstone Community Church held a cake fayre, and raised £45.32 to support its missionary, Helen Beck. The above photo recreates

the picture as it was submitted: dull, lifeless and very empty. It looks like a candid snapshot taken before the event has started. Look at this and compare it to the pictures that appear in your local newspaper – there is no way this could have been considered for printing. Had one of the organisers actually thought about it first, a proper photo opportunity could have been created – this is what we'll work towards.

The photographer is now standing on a chair, looking down at the cake fayre's organiser Karen Lyons. To try and create some drama, Karen is holding one of the cakes. But she's not smiling, making this a miserable picture. It could be better. The photographer has kneeled down to take this picture, and Karen is smiling. But look at the background – it's too busy! The first aid box looks as if it's growing out of her head.

By changing the angle at which the picture is taken, we've now got a usable picture – it looks as if there was a lot of cake, rather than three platefuls. But the background is still too busy.

This is the same picture, but using image editing software, the cluttered background has been removed.

However, this is the picture I would have submitted, as it has a clear focus: the eye goes down from Karen's smiling face to the cakes on the table – it instantly tells the story as there are no other details to divert your attention.

When you send a picture over to a newspaper, don't send it in without any explanation. The picture needs a caption: 'Karen Lyons, organiser of the Collinstone Cake Club, part of the Community Church, with some of the cakes sold to support the church's missionary Helen Beck. Picture taken by Matt Bugg.' Make sure you spell correctly the names of everyone in the picture, list them in the appropriate order ('from left, Karen Lyons …').

Avoid the shooting gallery

If you have a picture story that involves a row of people, don't take a picture of a row of people. Be inventive: if elders are welcoming a new minister, have them standing around the pastor. You could take a picture of the pastor from the pulpit with the congregation behind them. The line could be divided into two, arranged into a semicircle or the non-essential people taken out. But never take a picture of several people all in a row. It's the photographic equivalent of paint drying.

If you are holding an event

If you are holding an event in the church, think carefully about whether there is a photo opportunity at the event, or if one can be created. Whoever is going to take the picture needs to work out how it will be taken beforehand, possibly by visiting the venue first. If there's time to think, then there's time to be creative, which will always produce a better end result. If you're opening a new church building with a grand ribbon-cutting ceremony, then the obvious picture story is the ribbon being cut by the VIP guest. Time and again, people take pictures of the ribbon being cut from behind, from the side or after it's all happened. Instead of being haphazard and letting the picture be taken at the wrong time, from the wrong angle, why not be inventive? The snapper could be standing on the other side of the ribbon, so the picture is of the ribbon about to be cut by the VIP, surrounded by the crowds of people waiting to get in. Alternatively, someone could make a large pair of comedy scissors. If the VIP were to hold these next to the ribbon, it would make an eye-catching photograph – it need not be the actual ribbon cutting ceremony itself, just a prelude.

If you have time, do a dummy run of the pictures before the event, giving you the chance to work out the right angles and lighting. Make sure the organisers of the event know that you will be taking pictures and seek relevant permissions from people to photograph them.

Mugshots

Another useful tool in your church publicity kit is a good quality set of mugshots, ready to be sent to a newspaper or magazine when needed. What is a mugshot? It's a head and shoulders picture of someone, similar to a passport photo, although a good mugshot will resemble the person in the picture. While most pictures will be edited down to just the face and a bit of the neck, it's always a good idea to keep the shoulders in the picture – it gives any designer more flexibility. Keep the background neutral, such as a white wall or screen, so that the eye only focuses on the face – once the image has been tightened, you don't want it spoilt by having half a clock face coming out of an ear, or a flower growing out of the top of the head.

In case you hadn't noticed, people get older. Because time takes no prisoners, it's worth updating your gallery every year. Usually, you should only need a set of mugshots for the church leaders, be they the ministers, Parish Council or diaconate. If they are likely to speak to the press, then you'll need a mugshot for them on file. The best time to update your mugshot is probably after the church AGM has taken place and new officers appointed.

This is an example of a bad mugshot: it's blurred, there's something coming out of the subject's head and it's too dark. This mugshot chops off the top of the head and the shoulders and most of the face is in shadow, so it's unusable.

This is better, getting the whole head and shoulders in – but it's possibly a bit too 'stand to attention' and the background is busy.

Going inside, and a better angle. However, again the background is too busy, the plant could be going in one ear and out the other.

The neutral background improves the picture no end, but the screen divider creates a black line coming out of the head.

Here is a final version – the angle is interesting, the background is neutral, the shot is in focus and the subject doesn't look like he's on parade. The black line suggests how a newspaper would crop the picture.

Have fun

Photographs, more than anything, will offer a snapshot of what church is like. If we submit boring pictures with a press release, we will continue to reinforce negative impressions of the church. But by sending lively, happy pictures we give the opposite impression. So, take time to think about the impact your prints will have – if you have fun taking them, this will show and people will know that it's not dull following Jesus.

NOW IT'S YOUR TURN

Hopefully, this book has left you inspired to go out there and start ditching the day-glo. Church publicity has been a neglected ministry for far too long and I believe that, until now, it has been an underrated form of evangelism. The journey we've gone through during this book scratches the surface: where is the advice on producing posters for jumble sales? Or promoting your outreach events? Packing as much into this book has been hard, which is why I've developed the *Ditch the Day-glo* website (www.ditchthedayglo.co.uk). On it, you'll find additional help and articles relating to themes in this book, some downloads and some forums where you can all share your ideas and experiences with each other. You'll also be able to email me if you want some more helps and tips.

Let's grow this ministry together: in doing so, we'll be making inroads in the way that our neighbourhoods perceive the Church, and hopefully bring people to Christ.

APPENDIX:
A QUICK TYPOGRAPHY LESSON

One of my pet hates is poor typography: no wonder when I spent four years studying at Reading University and have worked in newspapers for over a decade. As you have now seen, typefaces – fonts, faces and type – set the mood for a printed piece of work. With thousands to choose from, getting the right type for the job is vital.

There are two main types of typefaces: serif and sans serif. This book is set in a serif typeface – the serifs are little flourishes that are at the end of each letter and sans serif typefaces don't have them.

There are other categories: slab (or Egyptian) serif faces have serifs that are the same width as the rest of the letter. There are also display faces, ideal for headlines and posters but not for distance reading, such as pages of a church magazine, or a hymnbook.

Even though there are thousands of typefaces, many churches stick to Comic Sans, Arial and Times New Roman.

Ditch the day-glo

A serif typeface

Ditch the day-glo

A sans-serif typeface

Ditch the day-glo

A slab serif typeface

DITCH THE DAY-GLO

A display typeface

Arial and Times are very boring as so many people use them, it's the typographical equivalent of everyone wearing brown overalls. Comic Sans, with its childish connotations, should never be used. This is why:

Ha! Ha! We're very sad to report the death of our longest serving member! She was 97! Ha! Ha! And she's been a member for a staggering 70 years! Ha! Ha!

Of course this is in poor taste: but this is the subliminal message we're sending out every time we use Comic Sans. Writing in *The Times*, Ian Peacock said, 'Comic Sans is the David Brent [from *The Office*] of typography: a failed office jester, desperately trying to be your pal.' Some argue that it's ideal for children. Studies by the University of Reading's department of typography and graphic communication found that, 'There is no research that says that either serif or sans serif typefaces are intrinsically more legible.' But children's reading comprehension is helped by an increased spacing (leading) between lines. Comic Sans is also sometimes suggested as an appropriate typeface for people with dyslexia, but opinion varies. Research suggests that better typefaces are available such as Sasoon, Read Regular and Lexia Readable. The latter is available to download free from www.k-fonts.com. It might seem frivolous to debunk Comic Sans, but never use it unless you really want the Church to come over as childish or comical.

Look at the typefaces that you have on your computer – try out each face with a sentence such as 'Typeface name: the quick brown fox jumps over the lazy dog', which contains every letter of the alphabet at least once. You'll need to print out each one to get a full favour of each face as the computer screen can distort them. Keep these printouts in a file and you'll be able to use it as a reference tool.

> Scala sans: The quick brown fox jumps over the lazy dog
> VICTORIA TITLING: THE QUICK BROWN FOX JUMPS OVER THE LAZY DOG

Having looked through the typefaces that came with your computer, you might not find one that gives the right impression of your fellowship. There are plenty of websites where you can download free typefaces, some come on the discs with computer magazines and there are often cheap CDs in computer stores. However, to get the best quality typefaces, its better to buy direct from a typeface foundry, such as Adobe or Monotype. Only buy the ones you want, and check the license restrictions: some will only be for up to five machines, something that should be adequate for most churches.

As you print out your 'quick brown foxes', you'll notice that some typefaces fit the sample text on one line, while others can't. Why is this when they are set at the same point size? Some typefaces have wider letters, making them less economical to use (at the same point size, you will get less words to a page). These wider faces might be just as legible at a smaller typesize, measured in points with 72 points to an inch. This is because the type has a larger x-height. A typeface's lower case letters are based around the height of the lower-case x. If it's taller, then it will be easier to read at smaller sizes:

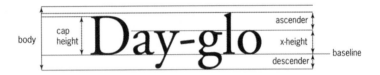

Here's how x-height makes a difference:

For God so loved the world that he gave his one and only Son, that whoever believes in him shall not perish but have eternal life. For God did not send his Son into the world to condemn the world, but to save the world through him. Whoever believes in him is not condemned, but whoever does not believe stands

For God so loved the world that he gave his one and only Son, that whoever believes in him shall not perish but have eternal life. For God did not send his Son into the world to condemn the world, but to save the world through him. Whoever believes in him

Times Roman and New Century Schoolbook set in 11 point text

For God so loved the world that he gave his one and only Son, that whoever believes in him shall not perish but have eternal life. For God did not send his Son into the world to condemn the world, but to save the world through him. Whoever believes in him is not condemned, but whoever does not believe stands

For God so loved the world that he gave his one and only Son, that whoever believes in him shall not perish but have eternal life. For God did not send his Son into the world to condemn the world, but to save the world through him. Whoever believes in him is not condemned, but whoever does not believe stands

Times Roman in 11 point text and New Century Schoolbook in 9 point

When both typefaces are set in 12 points, New Century Schoolbook looks much larger and doesn't fit the whole text in. When New Century Schoolbook is changed to 10 points, it looks as if it's the same size as Times New Roman at 12 points – it also packs the same amount of text in. This experimentation with typefaces might seem technical, but it's worthwhile, as you will find something that's distinctive and just right for your fellowship.

Legibility with typefaces isn't just down to the choice of typeface that you use. A lot of research has been carried out into how we read, essentially our eye reads by using the eye muscle to rotate the eyeball across a line of text. Like all muscles, it can get tired if it has to work too hard. So we can help it through several ways.

The first is to realise how you read. You might think that the eye recognises every letter and then forms them into words. But the eye reads groups of letters and research has proved that, as long as the first and last letters are in the right place, the letter order doesn't matter as much. The next set of diagrams shows how we rely on serifs to help us determine

hread   hrood

bread   brood

bread   **brood**

letter shapes. When we only have the top half of the letters we struggle to identify them – is it hrood, hread, bread, breed or brood? But with the lower half, we can make the distinctions needed to read.

Good typography also lets the eye muscle pace itself. As it moves across a line of text, it absorbs every word and eventually loses sight of the starting point. The word processing software I'm using gives me a line length of about 18 words a line. When my eye reaches the end of a line, my eyeball physically moves to the beginning of the next one. Making these judgements is tiring after a while. So the length of a line matters: the optimum line length is between nine and twelve words. Use columns or wider margins to achieve this.

The third way we can help our eye muscle is to set a comfortable spacing (leading) between the lines. Word processing software packages are the most inflexible at adjusting the leading, usually offering settings of 'normal' '1.5' or 'double'. However, adjusting the spacing manually can be useful. Have a look at the four examples opposite, both set in 10 point New Century Schoolbook again:

Even though the type is the same size, adjusting the leading makes a huge difference in how you perceive the text. A setting such as the last one (10pt on 14pt) is ideal for distance reading, such as a book or an academic paper.

And we know that in all things God works for the good of those who love him, who have been called according to his purpose. For those God foreknew he also predestined to be conformed to the likeness of his Son, that he might be the firstborn among many brothers.

New Century Schoolbook
10 point with 10 point leading

And those he predestined, he also called; those he called, he also justified; those he justified, he also glorified. What, then, shall we say in response to this? If God is for us, who can be against us? He who did not spare his own Son, but gave him up for us all—how will he not also, along with him, graciously give us all things?

New Century Schoolbook
10 point with 11 point leading

Who will bring any charge against those whom God has chosen? It is God who justifies. Who is he that condemns? Christ Jesus, who died—more than that, who was raised to life—is at the right hand of God and is also interceding for us. Who shall separate us from the love of Christ?

New Century Schoolbook
10 point with 12 point leading

Shall trouble or hardship or persecution or famine or nakedness or danger or sword? As it is written; "For your sake we face death all day long; we are considered as sheep to be slaughtered."

New Century Schoolbook
10 point with 14 point leading

There is more to typography than this, but follow these basics and you can't go far wrong. The best book to read to familiarise yourself with typography is the witty and very accessible *Stop Stealing Sheep and Find Out How Type Works,* by Erik Spiekermann and E.M. Ginger (Adobe Press).